THE

Designed to make Shakespeare's great plays available to all readers, the New Folger Library edition of Shakespeare's plays provides accurate texts in modern spelling and punctuation, as well as scene-by-scene action summaries, full explanatory notes, many pictures clarifying Shakespeare's language, and notes recording all significant departures from the early printed versions. Each play is prefaced by a brief introduction, by a guide to reading Shakespeare's language, and by accounts of his life and theater. Each play is followed by an annotated list of further readings and by a "Modern Perspective" written by an expert on that particular play.

Barbara A. Mowat is Director of Academic Programs at the Folger Shakespeare Library, Executive Editor of *Shakespeare Quarterly*, Chair of the Folger Institute, and author of *The Dramaturgy of Shakespeare's Romances* and of essays on Shakespeare's plays and on the editing of the plays.

Paul Werstine is Professor of English at the Graduate School and at King's University College at the University of Western Ontario. He is general editor of the New Variorum Shakespeare and author of many papers and articles on the printing and editing of Shakespeare's plays.

The Folger Shakespeare Library

The Folger Shakespeare Library in Washington, D.C., a privately funded research library dedicated to Shakespeare and the civilization of early modern Europe, was founded in 1932 by Henry Clay and Emily Jordan Folger. In addition to its role as the world's preeminent Shakespeare collection and its emergence as a leading center for Renaissance studies, the Folger Library offers a wide array of cultural and educational programs and services for the general public.

EDITORS

BARBARA A. MOWAT
Director of Academic Programs
Folger Shakespeare Library

PAUL WERSTINE
Professor of English
King's University College at the University of
Western Ontario, Canada

FOLGER Shakespeare Library

The Two Gentlemen of Verona

By
WILLIAM SHAKESPEARE

Edited by Barbara A. Mowat
and Paul Werstine

SIMON & SCHUSTER PAPERBACKS
New York London Toronto Sydney

Simon & Schuster Paperbacks
A Division of Simon & Schuster, Inc.
1230 Avenue of the Americas
New York, NY 10020

Copyright © 1999 by The Folger Shakespeare Library

All rights reserved, including the right to reproduce this book
or portions thereof in any form whatsoever. For information, address
Simon & Schuster Paperbacks Subsidiary Rights Department,
1230 Avenue of the Americas, New York, NY 10020.

Washington Square Press New Folger Edition December 1999
This Simon & Schuster paperback edition April 2009

SIMON & SCHUSTER PAPERBACKS and colophon are
registered trademarks of Simon & Schuster, Inc.

For information regarding special discounts for bulk purchases,
please contact Simon & Schuster Special Sales at
1-866-506-1949 or business@simonandschuster.com.

The Simon & Schuster Speakers Bureau can bring authors to your
live event. For more information or to book an event, contact the
Simon & Schuster Speakers Bureau at 1-866-248-3049 or visit our
website at www.simonspeakers.com.

Manufactured in the United States of America

10 9 8 7 6 5 4 3

ISBN 978-0-671-72295-1

From the Director of the Library

For over four decades, the Folger Library General Reader's Shakespeare provided accurate and accessible texts of the plays and poems to students, teachers, and millions of other interested readers. Today, in an age often impatient with the past, the passion for Shakespeare continues to grow. No author speaks more powerfully to the human condition, in all its variety, than this actor/playwright from a minor sixteenth-century English village.

Over the years vast changes have occurred in the way Shakespeare's works are edited, performed, studied, and taught. The New Folger Library Shakespeare replaces the earlier versions, bringing to bear the best and most current thinking concerning both the texts and their interpretation. Here is an edition which makes the plays and poems fully understandable for modern readers using uncompromising scholarship. Professors Barbara Mowat and Paul Werstine are uniquely qualified to produce this New Folger Shakespeare for a new generation of readers. The Library is grateful for the learning, clarity, and imagination they have brought to this ambitious project.

Werner Gundersheimer,
Director of the Folger Shakespeare Library
from 1984 to 2002

Contents

Editors' Preface

In recent years, ways of dealing with Shakespeare's texts and with the interpretation of his plays have been undergoing significant change. This edition, while retaining many of the features that have always made the Folger Shakespeare so attractive to the general reader, at the same time reflects these current ways of thinking about Shakespeare. For example, modern readers, actors, and teachers have become interested in the differences between, on the one hand, the early forms in which Shakespeare's plays were first published and, on the other hand, the forms in which editors through the centuries have presented them. In response to this interest, we have based our edition on what we consider the best early printed version of a particular play (explaining our rationale in a section called "An Introduction to This Text") and have marked our changes in the text—unobtrusively, we hope, but in such a way that the curious reader can be aware that a change has been made and can consult the "Textual Notes" to discover what appeared in the early printed version.

Current ways of looking at the plays are reflected in our brief prefaces, in many of the commentary notes, in the annotated lists of "Further Reading," and especially in each play's "Modern Perspective," an essay written by an outstanding scholar who brings to the reader his or her fresh assessment of the play in the light of today's interests and concerns.

As in the Folger Library General Reader's Shakespeare, which this edition replaces, we include explanatory notes designed to help make Shakespeare's language clearer to a modern reader, and we place the notes on the page facing the text that they explain. We also follow the earlier edition in including illustrations—of objects, of clothing, of mythological figures—from books and manuscripts in the Folger Library collection. We provide fresh accounts of the life of Shakespeare, of the publishing of his plays, and of the theaters in which his plays were performed, as well as an introduction to the text itself. We also include a section called "Reading Shakespeare's Language," in which we try to help readers learn to "break the code" of Elizabethan poetic language.

For each section of each volume, we are indebted to a host of generous experts and fellow scholars. The "Reading Shakespeare's Language" sections, for example, could not have been written had not Arthur King, of Brigham Young University, and Randall Robinson, author of *Unlocking Shakespeare's Language,* led the way in untangling Shakespearean language puzzles and shared their insights and methodologies generously with us. "Shakespeare's Life" profited by the careful reading given it by the late S. Schoenbaum, "Shakespeare's Theater" was read and strengthened by Andrew Gurr and John Astington, and "The Publication of Shakespeare's Plays" is indebted to the comments of Peter W. M. Blayney. We, as editors, take sole responsibility for any errors in our editions.

We are grateful to the authors of the "Modern Perspectives"; to Leeds Barroll and David Bevington for their generous encouragement; to the Huntington and Newberry Libraries for fellowship support; to King's College for the grants it has provided to Paul Werstine; to the Social Sciences and Humanities Research Council of Canada, which provided him with a Research Time Stipend for 1990–91; to Susan Snyder for helpful suggestions about this play; to Trevor Howard-Hill for allowing us to consult his preliminary commentary notes for the Variorum edition of *Two Gentlemen of Verona,* and to Carol Carlisle, his co-editor; to R. J.

Shroyer of the University of Western Ontario for essential computer support; to the Folger Institute's Center for Shakespeare Studies for its fortuitous sponsorship of a workshop on "Shakespeare's Texts for Students and Teachers" (funded by the National Endowment for the Humanities and led by Richard Knowles of the University of Wisconsin), a workshop from which we learned an enormous amount about what is wanted by college and high-school teachers of Shakespeare today; to Alice Falk for her expert copyediting; and especially to Steve Llano, our production editor at Pocket Books, whose expertise and attention to detail are essential to this project.

Our biggest debt is to the Folger Shakespeare Library—to Werner Gundersheimer, Director of the Library, who made possible our edition; to Deborah Curren-Aquino, who provides extensive editorial and production support; to Jean Miller, the Library's Art Curator, who combs the Library holdings for illustrations, and to Julie Ainsworth, Head of the Photography Department, who carefully photographs them; to Peggy O'Brien, former Director of Education at the Folger and now Director of Education Programs at the Corporation for Public Broadcasting, who gave us expert advice about the needs being expressed by Shakespeare teachers and students (and to Martha Christian and other "master teachers" who used our texts in manuscript in their classrooms); to Allan Shnerson for his expert computer support; to the staff of the Academic Programs Division, especially Rachel Kunkle (whose help has been crucial), Mary Tonkinson, Kathleen Lynch, Carol Brobeck, Toni Krieger, and Martha Fay; and, finally, to the generously supportive staff of the Library's Reading Room.

Barbara A. Mowat and Paul Werstine

Shakespeare's
The Two Gentlemen of Verona

Even though the word "gentlemen" in its title would suggest that this play's heroes are adults, the play is much more intelligible if we think of them as boys—boys who, as the play opens, are about to leave home on their own for the first time. Their longtime friendship has been dealt a double blow: one of the boys has developed a crush on a girl, though he hasn't yet told her that he likes her; the other is being sent off by his father to the equivalent of a boys' finishing school. In the course of the play's action, both boys make the journey away from home, and both behave in ways that get them in terrible trouble.

Sent to "the Emperor's court" in order to learn to be "perfect gentlemen"—to practice in "tilts and tournaments," to learn how to make proper (male) conversation—Valentine and then Proteus are in turn derailed by overwhelming attraction to Sylvia, the ruler's daughter. Valentine's characteristic gullibility and mental denseness do not deter Sylvia from returning his love, but these weaknesses do render him incapable of eloping with her without getting caught—and banished. Proteus' weaknesses—self-centeredness and the capacity for cold treachery—are triggered by his sudden love-at-first-sight desire for Valentine's girlfriend, a desire which wipes out his former love for Julia and leads him into committing a series of despicable acts that win from Sylvia nothing but scorn and that wound (but do not drive away) Julia, who has pursued him disguised as a boy. When Sylvia follows Valentine into banishment (and into the forest), and Proteus follows Sylvia, and

Julia follows Proteus, the stage is set for one of the more disturbing play-endings ever devised by Shakespeare. But the stage is also set for the play's "gentlemen" to begin to take small steps toward mature manhood.

Lest we not recognize the inner weaknesses that bedevil Valentine and Proteus, Shakespeare provides each with a servant who, either explicitly or by example, points out their failings. Speed is as bright as Valentine is dim, and when Valentine is fortunate enough to have Speed present to explain things to him, he functions not too badly. And Lance is as loving and compassionate as Proteus is callous. Lance's account of his farewell scene with his family—played out for the audience with the family roles represented by Lance's left and right shoes, his walking staff, and his dog Crab—is among the funniest scenes in Shakespeare; and Lance's later account of taking on himself the whippings earned by Crab (almost as funny as the "farewell" scene) comments pointedly, if indirectly and parodically, on Proteus' failures of loyalty.

It is often hard to know how a modern reader or spectator should respond to this play. The scenes with the outlaws in the forest seem to parody any number of things, though it is hard to say how the scenes would have been perceived by an audience in the 1590s. The disturbing actions in the play's final scene are hard to reconcile to today's views of "natural" sexual and social relationships—as Jeffrey Masten explains in the essay printed at the back of this book. But it helps to view Valentine and Proteus as boys struggling to keep their balance in the face of new and unexpected desires—making terrible errors but, with the help of staunchly loyal girlfriends, coming through to a livable future.

After you have read the play, we invite you to turn to the back of this book and read *"The Two Gentlemen of Verona:* A Modern Perspective," by Professor Jeffrey Masten of Northwestern University.

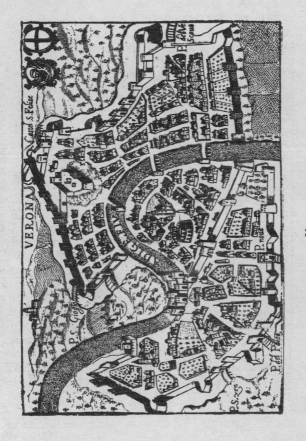

Verona.

From Pietro Bertelli, *Theatrum vrbium Italicarum . . .* (1599).

Milan. (1.1.63, 73)

From Pietro Bertelli, *Theatrum vrbium Italicarum . . .* (1599).

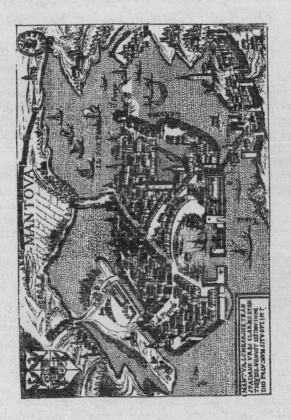

Mantua. (4.1.50, 4.3.25, 5.2.49)
From Pietro Bertelli, *Theatrum vrbium Italicarum . . .* (1599).

Reading Shakespeare's Language: *The Two Gentlemen of Verona*

For many people today, reading Shakespeare's language can be a problem—but it is a problem that can be solved. Those who have studied Latin (or even French or German or Spanish), and those who are used to reading poetry, will have little difficulty understanding the language of Shakespeare's poetic drama. Others, though, need to develop the skills of untangling unusual sentence structures and of recognizing and understanding poetic compressions, omissions, and wordplay. And even those skilled in reading unusual sentence structures may have occasional trouble with Shakespeare's words. Four hundred years of "static" intervene between his speaking and our hearing. Most of his immense vocabulary is still in use, but a few of his words are not, and, worse, some of his words now have meanings quite different from those they had in the sixteenth century. In the theater, most of these difficulties are solved for us by actors who study the language and articulate it for us so that the essential meaning is heard—or, when combined with stage action, is at least *felt*. When reading on one's own, one must do what each actor does: go over the lines (often with a dictionary close at hand) until the puzzles are solved and the lines yield up their poetry and the characters speak in words and phrases that are, suddenly, rewarding and wonderfully memorable.

Shakespeare's Words

As you begin to read the opening scenes of a play by Shakespeare, you may notice occasional unfamiliar words. Some are unfamiliar simply because we no longer use them. In the opening scenes of *Two Gentlemen of Verona*, for example, you will find the words *home-keeping* (i.e., stay-at-home), *sluggardized* (i.e., made lazy), *haply* (i.e., by chance), *parle* (i.e., conversation), and *angerly* (i.e., angrily). Words of this kind are explained in notes to the text and will become familiar the more of Shakespeare's plays you read.

In all of Shakespeare's writing, the more problematic words are those that we still use but that we use with a different meaning. In the opening scenes of *Two Gentlemen of Verona*, for example, the word *circumstance* has the meaning of "circumlocution," the word *blasting* is used where we would say "blighted," *watchful* where we would say "wakeful," *overcharged* where we would say "overcrowded," and *perceive* where we would say "obtain." Such words will be explained in the notes to the text, but they, too, will become familiar as you continue to read Shakespeare's language.

Some words are strange not because of the "static" introduced by changes in language over the past centuries but because these are words that Shakespeare is using to build a specific dramatic world. *Two Gentlemen of Verona*, for example, builds, in its opening scenes, a Petrarchan poetic world—a world, that is, in which the male lover presents himself as a worshiper of an almost divine mistress, linked to other desperate and famous lovers, speaking a special language of love. In *Two Gentlemen of Verona*, this world is constructed through references to "Love" (i.e., Cupid, the Roman god of love), to Leander and the Hellespont, and to a "love book"; to the lover who is "blasting in the bud," a "votary to fond desire"; and to a "fair resort of gentlemen" who "with parle" encounter sweet ʿadies. The play sets this world against one in which young men set out to seek for honor—constructed through references to the "road" (i.e., the harbor), to "hap" (i.e., fortune), to "grievance" (i.e., suffering, pain), to "wrack" (i.e., shipwreck), and to "tilts and tournaments."

Two Gentlemen of Verona differs from most of Shakespeare's plays in containing little language that builds a world with a recognizable space and time; indeed, some of the language (e.g., such words as "road" [meaning "harbor"], "shipped," and "wrack") cannot be associated with the real-world "Verona," which is inland. A comparable confusion surrounds the "court" to which Valentine (and then Proteus) travel, which is governed sometimes by an Emperor, sometimes by a Duke—and which is usually said to be in Milan, but is set once in Padua and once in Verona itself. The result is a placeless space in which young men are encouraged by their fathers and their own ambitions to seek honor but find themselves instead enmeshed in and driven by erotic desire.

Shakespeare's Sentences

In an English sentence, meaning is quite dependent on the place given each word. "The dog bit the boy" and "The boy bit the dog" mean very different things, even though the individual words are the same. Because English places such importance on the positions of words in sentences, on the way words are arranged, unusual arrangements can puzzle a reader. Shakespeare frequently shifts his sentences away from "normal" English arrangements—often to create the rhythm he seeks, sometimes to use a line's poetic rhythm to emphasize a particular word, sometimes to give a character his or her own speech patterns or to allow the character to speak in a special way. Again, when we attend a good performance of the play, the actors will have worked out the sentence structures and will articulate the sentences so that the meaning is clear. In reading for yourself, do as the actor does. That is, when you become puzzled by a character's speech, check to see if words are being presented in an unusual sequence.

Look first for the placement of subject and verb. Shakespeare often rearranges subjects and verbs (i.e., instead of "he goes," we find "goes he," or instead of "he does go" we find "does he go"). In *Two Gentlemen of Verona,* we find such a construction when Proteus says "Thus *have I shunned* the fire" (instead of "I have shunned"); he uses a similar construction when he later says "with the vantage of mine own excuse / *Hath he excepted* most against my love." Shakespeare also frequently places the object or the predicate adjective before the subject and verb (i.e., instead of "I hit him," we might find "him I hit," and instead of "It is blue," we might find "Blue it is"). Antonio's "Like exhibition thou shalt have from me" is an example of such an inversion (with the object, "Like exhibition," preceding the subject and verb), as is Lucetta's "melodious were it, would you sing it" (where, instead of "it were [i.e., would be] melodious," the predicate adjective precedes the verb, which in turn precedes the subject). In this very early play, inversions serve primarily to shape and control the rhythm of the line, though occasionally (as in Antonio's "Like exhibition thou shalt have from me") the inversion also shifts the emphasis to the object.

Inversions are not the only unusual sentence structures in Shakespeare's language. Often in his sentences words that would normally appear together are separated from each other. (Again, this is often done to create a particular rhythm or to stress a particular word.) Take, for example, Lucetta's "'tis a passing shame / That *I*, unworthy body as I am, / *Should censure* thus on lovely gentlemen." Here the noun phrase "unworthy body as I am" separates the subject "I" from its verb "Should censure." Or take Valentine's "I *will write*, / Please you command, *a thousand times as much*," where the clause "Please you command" separates the verb "will write" from its object, "a thousand times as much." In order to create for yourself sentences that seem more like the English of everyday speech, you may wish to rearrange the words, putting together the word clusters ("that I should censure," "I will write a thousand times as much"). You will usually find that the sentence will gain in clarity but will lose its rhythm or shift its emphasis.

In many of Shakespeare's plays, sentences are sometimes complicated not because of unusual structures or interruptions but because Shakespeare omits words and parts of words that English sentences normally require. (In conversation, we, too, often omit words. We say, "Heard from him yet?" and our hearer supplies the missing "Have you.") Frequent reading of Shakespeare—and of other poets—trains us to supply such missing words. In his later plays, Shakespeare uses omissions both of verbs and of nouns to great dramatic effect. In *Two Gentlemen of Verona* omissions seem to be used primarily for the sake of the rhythm of the line. For example, in Julia's "What fool is she that knows I am a maid," the omission of the word "a" before "fool" allows a regular iambic pentameter line to be created.

Shakespearean Wordplay

Shakespeare plays with language so often and so variously that entire books are written on the topic. Here we will mention only three kinds of wordplay: puns, metaphors, and similes. A pun is a play on words that sound the same but have different meanings (or on a single word that has more than one meaning). Much of the dialogue in *Two Gentlemen of Verona* is based on puns and related kinds of wordplay. In the opening conversation between Proteus and Valentine, for example, a reference to the Hellespont (a strait that links the Sea of Marmora and the Aegean Sea) leads to Valentine's charge that Proteus, though he "never swam the Hellespont," is "over boots in love" (1.1.25–26). Here, "over boots in" means both "up to the ankles in" and "recklessly committed to pursuing." Proteus responds with a proverbial saying, "give me not the boots," which means, in effect, "don't make a fool of me," and which may contain an additional pun on "the boots," a Scottish instrument of torture used to extort confessions from prisoners. Valentine in turn adds a final pun on "boots," saying "it boots thee not" ("boots" here being a verb meaning "profits").

To give only one other example from hundreds available in this play: In 2.1, Speed lists the symptoms that reveal Valentine's lovelorn state. When Valentine asks "Are all these things perceived in me?" Speed answers "They are all perceived without you," introducing a set of multiple puns on the word "without" (lines 34–41). Speed's "without you" probably means "in your appearance and behavior" (or, more literally, "on your exterior"). However, the phrase "without you" usually meant (and still usually means) "in your absence," and this is the meaning that the phrase seems to have in Valentine's

puzzled reply to Speed: "Without me? They cannot,"
i.e., "This appearance and behavior *cannot* be perceived
in me in my absence." Having baffled Valentine with the
pun on *without*, Speed then puns again and again on the
same word: "Without you? Nay, that's certain, for without you were so simple [i.e., if you were not so simple],
none else would [i.e., would perceive them]. But you are
so without [i.e., so much on the outside of] these follies,
that these follies are within you. . . ." Such intricate
punning is so characteristic of the language of this play
that one must listen (or read) with care if one hopes to
follow the dialogue's twists and turns.

Metaphors and similes are plays on words in which
one object or idea is expressed as if it were something
else, something with which it shares common features.
Proteus, for example, uses a metaphor to describe his
situation near the end of 1.3. He has entered the scene
reading a letter from his beloved Julia and unexpectedly
has encountered his father. Seeking to conceal his
relationship with Julia from his father, he has said that
the letter was from Valentine, who wished that Proteus
were with him at the Emperor's court. Proteus' father,
accepting his son's misrepresentations of the letter, has
ordered Proteus to leave Verona to join Valentine. Alone
onstage after this unwelcome dialogue with his father,
Proteus presents his plight in a metaphor: "Thus have I
shunned the fire for fear of burning / And drenched me
in the sea, where I am drowned" (79–80)—"the fire"
being the feared discovery of his love for Julia and "the
sea" the parental order for him to leave Verona.

Julia, preparing to journey to Milan to find Proteus,
uses a series of metaphors to embody her emotional
states (2.7.15–38). Urged to wait for Proteus' return, she
makes literal the emotional hunger she feels by asking
"O, know'st thou not his looks are my soul's food? / Pity
the dearth that I have pinèd in / By longing for that food

so long a time." The metaphor of "love is a hunger that must be fed" then shifts to "love is a fire that can't be quenched," and then to "love is a stream that must not be dammed," and finally to "the lover who finds the beloved is a blessed soul resting in Elysium."

Frequently in *Two Gentlemen of Verona* the metaphoric wordplay takes the form of similes, with "as" or "like" used to connect the terms of the comparison. When Julia is left alone onstage in 1.2, for example, she uses a simile to share with the audience her confusion about her mixed responses to Proteus' letter, comparing her lovelorn self to a fretful infant: "Fie, fie, how wayward is this foolish love / That like a testy babe will scratch the nurse / And presently, all humbled, kiss the rod!" (lines 60–62). In 2.4 Proteus abandons Julia for Sylvia with a series of similes that form an analogy. "Even as one heat another heat expels, / Or as one nail by strength drives out another, / So the remembrance of my former love / Is by a newer object quite forgotten" (lines 202–5). A few lines later in the speech, he again turns to simile to describe to himself his new emotional state: "now my love is thawed, / Which like a waxen image 'gainst a fire / Bears no impression of the thing it was" (lines 210–12).

Implied Stage Action

Finally, in reading Shakespeare's plays we should always remember that what we are reading is a performance script. The dialogue is written to be spoken by actors who, at the same time, are moving, gesturing, picking up objects, weeping, shaking their fists. Some stage action is described in what are called "stage directions"; some is suggested within the dialogue itself. We must learn to be alert to such signals as we stage the play in our imaginations. When, in *Two Gentlemen of Verona* 1.2.34–36, Lucetta says to Julia "Peruse this paper, madam," and Julia in turn says " 'To Julia.'—Say from whom," it is obvious that Lucetta has handed a paper to Julia. Again, in 2.2.5–6, when Julia says "Keep this remembrance for thy Julia's sake," and Proteus replies "Why, then we'll make exchange. Here, take you this," it is equally clear that the two exchange love tokens.

Occasionally in *Two Gentlemen of Verona*, signals to the reader are not so obvious. For example, in 4.2 the Folio text does not make clear who sings the song to Sylvia or precisely how the complicated action is to be rendered. One scholar has proposed that the music be sung offstage while the Host and Julia talk alone onstage, and that Sylvia then enter through a central door instead of entering "above" at her window, as the scene is normally staged. As editors we have chosen to suggest that Proteus sing the song, that the musicians remain onstage during their performance, and that Sylvia enter "above"; but readers, directors, and actors may want to stage the scene differently, either in their own imaginations or onstage. Learning to read the language of stage action repays one many times over when one encounters a scene like that of Julia's dialogue with the pieces of Proteus' torn-up love letter (1.2) or that of Lance's enactment of his family's farewell scene, in which the family roles are represented by Lance's two shoes, his staff, and his dog Crab (2.3).

It is immensely rewarding to work carefully with Shakespeare's language so that the words, the sentences, the wordplay, and the implied stage action all become clear—as readers for the past four centuries have discovered. It may be more pleasurable to attend a good performance of a play—though not everyone has thought so. But the joy of being able to stage one of Shakespeare's plays in one's imagination, to return to passages that continue to yield further meanings (or further questions) the more one reads them—these are pleasures that, for many, rival (or at least augment) those of the performed text, and certainly make it worth considerable effort to "break the code" of Elizabethan poetic drama and let free the remarkable language that makes up a Shakespeare text.

Shakespeare's Life

Surviving documents that give us glimpses into the life of William Shakespeare show us a playwright, poet, and actor who grew up in the market town of Stratford-upon-Avon, spent his professional life in London, and returned to Stratford a wealthy landowner. He was born in April 1564, died in April 1616, and is buried inside the chancel of Holy Trinity Church in Stratford.

We wish we could know more about the life of the world's greatest dramatist. His plays and poems are testaments to his wide reading—especially to his knowledge of Virgil, Ovid, Plutarch, Holinshed's *Chronicles*, and the Bible—and to his mastery of the English language, but we can only speculate about his education. We know that the King's New School in Stratford-upon-Avon was considered excellent. The school was one of the English "grammar schools" established to educate young men, primarily in Latin grammar and literature. As in other schools of the time, students began their studies at the age of four or five in the attached "petty school," and there learned to read and write in English, studying primarily the catechism from the Book of Common Prayer. After two years in the petty school, students entered the lower form (grade) of the grammar school, where they began the serious study of Latin grammar and Latin texts that would occupy most of the remainder of their school days. (Several Latin texts that Shakespeare used repeatedly in writing his plays and poems were texts that schoolboys memorized and recited.) Latin comedies were introduced early in the lower form; in the upper form, which the boys entered at age ten or eleven, students wrote their own Latin orations and declamations, studied Latin historians and rhetoricians, and began the study of Greek using the Greek New Testament.

Since the records of the Stratford "grammar school" do not survive, we cannot prove that William Shakespeare attended the school; however, every indication (his father's position as an alderman and bailiff of Stratford, the playwright's own knowledge of the Latin classics, scenes in the plays that recall grammar-school experiences—for example, *The Merry Wives of Windsor*, 4.1) suggests that he did. We also lack generally accepted documentation about Shakespeare's life after his schooling ended and his professional life in London began. His marriage in 1582 (at age eighteen) to Anne Hathaway and the subsequent births of his daughter Susanna (1583) and the twins Judith and Hamnet (1585) are recorded, but how he supported himself and where he lived are not known. Nor do we know when and why he left Stratford for the London theatrical world, nor how he rose to be the important figure in that world that he had become by the early 1590s.

We do know that by 1592 he had achieved some prominence in London as both an actor and a playwright. In that year was published a book by the playwright Robert Greene attacking an actor who had the audacity to write blank-verse drama and who was "in his own conceit [i.e., opinion] the only Shake-scene in a country." Since Greene's attack includes a parody of a line from one of Shakespeare's early plays, there is little doubt that it is Shakespeare to whom he refers, a "Shake-scene" who had aroused Greene's fury by successfully competing with university-educated dramatists like Greene himself. It was in 1593 that Shakespeare became a published poet. In that year he published his long narrative poem *Venus and Adonis;* in 1594, he followed it with *The Rape of Lucrece.* Both poems were dedicated to the young earl of Southampton (Henry Wriothesley), who may have become Shakespeare's patron.

It seems no coincidence that Shakespeare wrote these narrative poems at a time when the theaters were closed because of the plague, a contagious epidemic disease that devastated the population of London. When the theaters reopened in 1594, Shakespeare apparently resumed his double career of actor and playwright and began his long (and seemingly profitable) service as an acting-company shareholder. Records for December of 1594 show him to be a leading member of the Lord Chamberlain's Men. It was this company of actors, later named the King's Men, for whom he would be a principal actor, dramatist, and shareholder for the rest of his career.

So far as we can tell, that career spanned about twenty years. In the 1590s, he wrote his plays on English history as well as several comedies and at least two tragedies (*Titus Andronicus* and *Romeo and Juliet*). These histories, comedies, and tragedies are the plays credited to him in 1598 in a work, *Palladis Tamia,* that in one chapter compares English writers with "Greek, Latin, and Italian Poets." There the author, Francis Meres, claims that Shakespeare is comparable to the Latin dramatists Seneca for tragedy and Plautus for comedy, and calls him "the most excellent in both kinds for the stage." He also names him "Mellifluous and

CATECHISMVS

paruus pueris primùm Latinè
qui ediscatur, proponendus
in Scholis.

LONDINI
Apud Iohannem Dayum Typo-
graphum. An. 1573.

Cum Priuilegio Regiæ Maiestatis.

Title page of a 1573 Latin and Greek catechism
for children.

honey-tongued Shakespeare": "I say," writes Meres, "that the Muses would speak with Shakespeare's fine filed phrase, if they would speak English." Since Meres also mentions Shakespeare's "sugared sonnets among his private friends," it is assumed that many of Shakespeare's sonnets (not published until 1609) were also written in the 1590s.

In 1599, Shakespeare's company built a theater for themselves across the river from London, naming it the Globe. The plays that are considered by many to be Shakespeare's major tragedies (*Hamlet, Othello, King Lear,* and *Macbeth*) were written while the company was resident in this theater, as were such comedies as *Twelfth Night* and *Measure for Measure.* Many of Shakespeare's plays were performed at court (both for Queen Elizabeth I and, after her death in 1603, for King James I), some were presented at the Inns of Court (the residences of London's legal societies), and some were doubtless performed in other towns, at the universities, and at great houses when the King's Men went on tour; otherwise, his plays from 1599 to 1608 were, so far as we know, performed only at the Globe. Between 1608 and 1612, Shakespeare wrote several plays—among them *The Winter's Tale* and *The Tempest*—presumably for the company's new indoor Blackfriars theater, though the plays seem to have been performed also at the Globe and at court. Surviving documents describe a performance of *The Winter's Tale* in 1611 at the Globe, for example, and performances of *The Tempest* in 1611 and 1613 at the royal palace of Whitehall.

Shakespeare wrote very little after 1612, the year in which he probably wrote *King Henry VIII.* (It was at a performance of *Henry VIII* in 1613 that the Globe caught fire and burned to the ground.) Sometime between 1610 and 1613 he seems to have returned to live in Stratford-upon-Avon, where he owned a large house and considerable property, and where his wife and his two daughters and their husbands lived. (His son Hamnet had died in 1596.) During his professional years in London, Shakespeare had presumably derived income from the acting company's profits as well as from his own career as an actor, from the sale of his play manuscripts to the acting company, and, after 1599, from his shares as an owner of the Globe. It was presumably that income, carefully invested in land and other property, which made him the wealthy man that surviving documents show him to have become. It is also assumed that William Shakespeare's growing wealth and reputation played some part in inclining the crown, in 1596, to grant John Shakespeare, William's father, the coat of arms that he had so long sought. William Shakespeare died in Stratford on April 23, 1616 (according to the epitaph carved under his bust in Holy Trinity Church) and was buried on April 25. Seven years after his death, his collected plays were published as *Mr. William Shakespeares Comedies, Histories, & Tragedies* (the work now known as the First Folio).

The years in which Shakespeare wrote were among the most exciting in English history. Intellectually, the discovery, translation, and printing of Greek and Roman classics were making available a set of works and worldviews that interacted complexly with Christian texts and beliefs. The result was a questioning, a vital intellectual ferment, that provided energy for the period's amazing dramatic and literary output and that fed directly into Shakespeare's plays. The Ghost in *Hamlet*, for example, is wonderfully complicated in part because he is a figure from Roman tragedy—the spirit of the dead returning to seek revenge—who at the same time inhabits a Christian hell (or purgatory); Hamlet's description of humankind reflects at one moment the

The Globe

A stylized representation of the Globe theater.
From Claes Jansz Visscher, *Londinum florentissima
Britanniae urbs* . . . [c. 1625].

Neoplatonic wonderment at mankind ("What a piece of work is a man!") and, at the next, the Christian disparagement of human sinners ("And yet, to me, what is this quintessence of dust?").

As intellectual horizons expanded, so also did geographical and cosmological horizons. New worlds—both North and South America—were explored, and in them were found human beings who lived and worshiped in ways radically different from those of Renaissance Europeans and Englishmen. The universe during these years also seemed to shift and expand. Copernicus had earlier theorized that the earth was not the center of the cosmos but revolved as a planet around the sun. Galileo's telescope, created in 1609, allowed scientists to see that Copernicus had been correct; the universe was not organized with the earth at the center, nor was it so nicely circumscribed as people had, until that time, thought. In terms of expanding horizons, the impact of these discoveries on people's beliefs—religious, scientific, and philosophical—cannot be overstated.

London, too, rapidly expanded and changed during the years (from the early 1590s to around 1610) that Shakespeare lived there. London—the center of England's government, its economy, its royal court, its overseas trade—was, during these years, becoming an exciting metropolis, drawing to it thousands of new citizens every year. Troubled by overcrowding, by poverty, by recurring epidemics of the plague, London was also a mecca for the wealthy and the aristocratic, and for those who sought advancement at court, or power in government or finance or trade. One hears in Shakespeare's plays the voices of London—the struggles for power, the fear of venereal disease, the language of buying and selling. One hears as well the voices of Stratford-upon-Avon—references to the nearby Forest of Arden, to sheepherding, to small-town gossip, to village fairs and markets. Part of the richness of Shakespeare's work is the influence felt there of the various worlds in which he lived: the world of metropolitan London, the world of small-town and rural England, the world of the theater, and the worlds of craftsmen and shepherds.

That Shakespeare inhabited such worlds we know from surviving London and Stratford documents, as well as from the evidence of the plays and poems themselves. From such records we can sketch the dramatist's life. We know from his works that he was a voracious reader. We know from legal and business documents that he was a multifaceted theater man who became a wealthy landowner. We know a bit about his family life and a fair amount about his legal and financial dealings. Most scholars today depend upon such evidence as they draw their picture of the world's greatest playwright. Such, however, has not always been the case. Until the late eighteenth century, the William Shakespeare who lived in most biographies was the creation of legend and tradition. This was the Shakespeare who was supposedly caught poaching deer at Charlecote, the estate of Sir Thomas Lucy close by Stratford; this was the Shakespeare who fled from Sir Thomas' vengeance and made his way in London by taking care of horses outside a playhouse; this was the Shakespeare who reportedly could barely read but whose natural gifts were extraordinary, whose father was a butcher who allowed his gifted son sometimes to help in the butcher shop, where William supposedly killed calves "in a high style," making a speech for the occasion. It was this legendary William Shakespeare whose Falstaff (in *1* and *2 Henry IV*) so pleased Queen Elizabeth that she demanded a play about Falstaff in love, and demanded that it be written in fourteen days (hence the existence of *The Merry Wives of Windsor*). It

"There shall he practice tilts and tournaments." (1.3.31)

Der Quintain

From Theodor Graminaeus, *Beschreibung derer fürstlicher güligscher . . .* (1587).

was this legendary Shakespeare who reached the top of his acting career in the roles of the Ghost in *Hamlet* and old Adam in *As You Like It*—and who died of a fever contracted by drinking too hard at "a merry meeting" with the poets Michael Drayton and Ben Jonson. This legendary Shakespeare is a rambunctious, undisciplined man, as attractively "wild" as his plays were seen by earlier generations to be. Unfortunately, there is no trace of evidence to support these wonderful stories.

Perhaps in response to the disreputable Shakespeare of legend—or perhaps in response to the fragmentary and, for some, all-too-ordinary Shakespeare documented by surviving records—some people since the mid–nineteenth century have argued that William Shakespeare could not have written the plays that bear his name. These persons have put forward some dozen names as more likely authors, among them Queen Elizabeth, Sir Francis Bacon, Edward de Vere (earl of Oxford), and Christopher Marlowe. Such attempts to find what for these people is a more believable author of the plays is a tribute to the regard in which the plays are held. Unfortunately for their claims, the documents that exist that provide evidence for the facts of Shakespeare's life tie him inextricably to the body of plays and poems that bear his name. Unlikely as it seems to those who want the works to have been written by an aristocrat, a university graduate, or an "important" person, the plays and poems seem clearly to have been produced by a man from Stratford-upon-Avon with a very good "grammar-school" education and a life of experience in London and in the world of the London theater. How this particular man produced the works that dominate the cultures of much of the world almost four hundred years after his death is one of life's mysteries—and one that will continue to tease our imaginations as we continue to delight in his plays and poems.

Shakespeare's Theater

The actors of Shakespeare's time are known to have performed plays in a great variety of locations. They played at court (that is, in the great halls of such royal residences as Whitehall, Hampton Court, and Greenwich); they played in halls at the universities of Oxford and Cambridge, and at the Inns of Court (the residences in London of the legal societies); and they also played in the private houses of great lords and civic officials. Sometimes acting companies went on tour from London into the provinces, often (but not only) when outbreaks of bubonic plague in the capital forced the closing of theaters to reduce the possibility of contagion in crowded audiences. In the provinces the actors usually staged their plays in churches (until around 1600) or in guildhalls. While surviving records show only a handful of occasions when actors played at inns while on tour, London inns were important playing places up until the 1590s.

The building of theaters in London had begun only shortly before Shakespeare wrote his first plays in the 1590s. These theaters were of two kinds: outdoor or public playhouses that could accommodate large numbers of playgoers, and indoor or private theaters for much smaller audiences. What is usually regarded as the first London outdoor public playhouse was called simply the Theatre. James Burbage—the father of Richard Burbage, who was perhaps the most famous actor in Shakespeare's company—built it in 1576 in an area north of the city of London called Shoreditch. Among the more famous of the other public playhouses that capitalized on the new fashion were the Curtain and the Fortune (both also built north of the city), the Rose, the Swan, the Globe, and the Hope (all located on the Bankside, a region just across the Thames south of the city of London). All these playhouses had to be built outside the jurisdiction of the city of London because many civic officials were hostile to the performance of drama and repeatedly petitioned the royal council to abolish it.

The theaters erected on the Bankside (a region under the authority of the Church of England, whose head was the monarch) shared the neighborhood with houses of prostitution and with the Paris Garden, where the blood sports of bearbaiting and bullbaiting were carried on. There may have been no clear distinction between playhouses and buildings for such sports, for we know that the Hope was used for both plays and baiting and that Philip Henslowe, owner of the Rose and, later, partner in the ownership of the Fortune, was also a partner in a monopoly on baiting. All these forms of entertainment were easily accessible to Londoners by boat across the Thames or over London Bridge.

Evidently Shakespeare's company prospered on the Bankside. They moved there in 1599. Threatened by difficulties in renewing the lease on the land where their first theater (the Theatre) had been built, Shakespeare's company took advantage of the Christmas holiday in 1598 to dismantle the Theatre and transport its timbers across the Thames to the Bankside, where, in 1599, these timbers were used in the building of the Globe. The weather in late December 1598 is recorded as having been especially harsh. It was so cold that the Thames was "nigh [nearly] frozen," and there was heavy snow. Perhaps the weather aided Shakespeare's company in eluding their landlord, the snow hiding their activity and the freezing of the Thames allowing them to slide the timbers across to the Bankside without paying tolls for repeated trips over London Bridge. Attractive as this narrative is, it remains just as likely that the heavy snow hampered transport of the timbers in wagons through the London streets to the river. It also must be remembered that the Thames was, according to report, only "nigh frozen" and therefore as impassable as it ever was. Whatever the precise circumstances of this fascinating event in English theater history, Shakespeare's company was able to begin playing at their new Globe theater on the Bankside in 1599. After the first Globe burned down in 1613 during the staging of Shakespeare's *Henry VIII* (its thatch roof was set alight by cannon fire called for by the performance), Shakespeare's company immediately rebuilt on the same location. The second Globe seems to have been a grander structure than its predecessor. It remained in use until the beginning of the English Civil War in 1642, when Parliament officially closed the theaters. Soon thereafter it was pulled down.

The public theaters of Shakespeare's time were very different buildings from our theaters today. First of all, they were open-air playhouses. As recent excavations of the Rose and the Globe confirm, some were polygonal or roughly circular in shape; the Fortune, however, was square. The most recent estimates of their size put the diameter of these buildings at 72 feet (the Rose) to 100 feet (the Globe), but we know that they held vast audiences of two or three thousand, who must have been squeezed together quite tightly. Some of these spectators paid extra to sit or stand in the two or three levels of roofed galleries that extended, on the upper levels, all the way around the theater and surrounded an open space. In this space were the stage and, perhaps, the tiring house (what we would call dressing rooms), as well as the so-called yard. In the yard stood the spectators who chose to pay less, the ones whom Hamlet contemptuously called "groundlings." For a roof they had only the sky, and so they were exposed to all kinds of weather. They stood on a floor that was sometimes made of mortar and sometimes of ash mixed with the shells of hazelnuts. The latter provided a porous and therefore dry footing for the crowd, and the shells may have been more comfortable to stand on because they were not as hard as mortar. Availability of shells may not have been a problem if hazelnuts were a favorite food for Shakespeare's audiences to munch on as they watched his plays. Archaeologists who are today unearthing the remains of theaters from this period have discovered quantities of these nutshells on theater sites.

Unlike the yard, the stage itself was covered by a roof. Its ceiling, called "the heavens," is thought to have been elaborately painted to depict the sun, moon, stars, and planets. Just how big the stage was remains hard to determine. We have a single sketch of part of the interior of the Swan. A Dutchman named Johannes de Witt visited this theater around 1596 and sent a sketch of it back to his friend, Arend van Buchel. Because van Buchel found de Witt's letter and sketch of interest, he copied both into a book. It is van Buchel's copy, adapted, it seems, to the shape and size of the page in his book, that survives. In this sketch, the stage appears to be a large rectangular platform that thrusts far out into the yard, perhaps even as far as the center of the circle formed by the surrounding galleries. This drawing, combined with the specifications for the size of the stage in the building contract for the Fortune, has led scholars to conjecture that the stage on which Shakespeare's plays were performed must have measured approximately 43 feet in width and 27 feet in depth, a vast acting area. But the digging up of a large part of the Rose by archaeologists has provided evidence of a quite different stage design. The Rose stage was a platform tapered at the corners and much shallower than what seems to be depicted in the van Buchel sketch. Indeed, its measurements seem to be about 37.5 feet across at its widest point and only 15.5 feet deep. Because the surviving indications of stage size and design differ from each other so much, it is possible that the stages in other theaters, like the Theatre, the Curtain, and the Globe (the outdoor playhouses where we know that Shakespeare's plays were performed), were different from those at both the Swan and the Rose.

After about 1608 Shakespeare's plays were staged not only at the Globe but also at an indoor or private playhouse in Blackfriars. This theater had been constructed in 1596 by James Burbage in an upper hall of a former Dominican priory or monastic house. Although Henry VIII had dissolved all English monasteries in the 1530s (shortly after he had founded the Church of England), the area remained under church, rather than hostile civic, control. The hall that Burbage had purchased and renovated was a large one in which Parliament had once met. In the private theater that he constructed, the stage, lit by candles, was built across the narrow end of the hall, with boxes flanking it. The rest of the hall offered seating room only. Because there was no provision for standing room, the largest audience it could hold was less than a thousand, or about a quarter of what the Globe could accommodate. Admission to Blackfriars was correspondingly more expensive. Instead of a penny to stand in the yard at the Globe, it cost a minimum of sixpence to get into Blackfriars. The best seats at the Globe (in the Lords' Room in the gallery above and behind the stage) cost sixpence; but the boxes flanking the stage at Blackfriars were half a crown, or five times sixpence. Some spectators who were particularly interested in displaying themselves paid even more to sit on stools on the Blackfriars stage.

Whether in the outdoor or indoor playhouses, the stages of Shakespeare's time were different from ours. They were not separated from the audience by the dropping of a curtain between acts and scenes. Therefore the playwrights of the time had to find other ways of signaling to the audience that one scene (to be imagined as occurring in one location at a given time) had ended and the next (to be imagined at perhaps a different location at a later time) had begun. The customary way used by Shakespeare and many of his contemporaries was to have everyone onstage exit at the end of one scene and have one or more different characters enter to begin the next. In a few cases, where characters remain onstage from one scene to another, the dialogue or stage action makes the change of location clear, and the characters are generally to be imagined as having moved from one place to another. For example, in *Romeo and Juliet*, Romeo and his friends remain onstage in Act 1 from scene 4 to scene 5, but they are represented as having moved between scenes from the street that leads to Capulet's house into Capulet's house itself. The new location is signaled in part by the appearance onstage of Capulet's servingmen carrying napkins, something they would not take into the streets. Playwrights had to be quite resourceful in the use of hand properties, like the napkin, or in the use of dialogue to specify where the action was taking place in their plays because, in contrast to most of today's theaters, the playhouses of Shakespeare's time did not use movable scenery to dress the stage and make the setting precise. As another consequence of this difference, however, the playwrights of Shakespeare's time did not have to specify exactly where the action of their plays was set when they did not choose to do so, and much of the action of their plays is tied to no specific place.

Usually Shakespeare's stage is referred to as a "bare stage," to distinguish it from the stages of the last two or three centuries with their elaborate sets. But the stage in Shakespeare's time was not completely bare. Philip Henslowe, owner of the Rose, lists in his inventory of stage properties a rock, three tombs, and two mossy banks. Stage directions in plays of the time also call for such things as thrones (or "states"), banquets (presumably tables with plaster replicas of food on them), and beds and tombs to be pushed onto the stage. Thus the stage often held more than the actors.

The actors did not limit their performing to the stage alone. Occasionally they went beneath the stage, as the Ghost appears to do in the first act of *Hamlet*. From there they could emerge onto the stage through a trapdoor. They could retire behind the hangings across the back of the stage (or the front of the tiring house), as, for example, the actor playing Polonius does when he hides behind the arras. Sometimes the hangings could be drawn back during a performance to "discover" one or more actors behind them. When performance required that an actor appear "above," as when Juliet is imagined to stand at the window of her chamber in the famous and misnamed "balcony scene," then the actor probably climbed the stairs to the gallery over the back of the stage and temporarily shared it with some of the spectators. The stage was also provided with ropes and winches so that actors could descend from, and reascend to, the "heavens."

Perhaps the greatest difference between dramatic performances in Shakespeare's time and ours was that in Shakespeare's England the roles of women were played by boys. (Some of these boys grew up to take male roles in their maturity.) There were no women in the acting companies, only in the audience. It had not always been so in the history of the English stage. There are records of women on English stages in the thirteenth and fourteenth centuries, two hundred years before Shakespeare's plays were performed. After the accession of James I in 1603, the queen of England and her ladies took part in entertainments at court called masques, and with the reopening of the theaters in 1660 at the restoration of Charles II, women again took their place on the public stage.

The chief competitors for the companies of adult actors such as the one to which Shakespeare belonged and for which he wrote were companies of exclusively boy actors. The competition was most intense in the early 1600s. There were then two principal children's companies: the Children of Paul's (the choirboys from St. Paul's Cathedral, whose private playhouse was near the cathedral); and the Children of the Chapel Royal (the choirboys from the monarch's private chapel, who performed at the Blackfriars theater built by Burbage in 1596, which Shakespeare's company had been stopped from using by local residents who objected to crowds). In *Hamlet* Shakespeare writes of "an aerie [nest] of children, little eyases [hawks], that cry out on the top of question and are most tyrannically clapped for 't. These are now the fashion and . . . berattle the common stages [attack the public theaters]." In the long run, the adult actors prevailed. The Children of Paul's dissolved around 1606. By about 1608 the Children of the Chapel Royal had been forced to stop playing at the Blackfriars theater, which was then taken over by the King's Men, Shakespeare's own troupe.

Acting companies and theaters of Shakespeare's time were organized in different ways. For example, Philip

Henslowe owned the Rose and leased it to companies of actors, who paid him from their takings. Henslowe would act as manager of these companies, initially paying playwrights for their plays and buying properties, recovering his outlay from the actors. Shakespeare's company, however, managed itself, with the principal actors, Shakespeare among them, having the status of "sharers" and the right to a share in the takings, as well as the responsibility for a part of the expenses. Five of the sharers themselves, Shakespeare among them, owned the Globe. As actor, as sharer in an acting company and in ownership of theaters, and as playwright, Shakespeare was about as involved in the theatrical industry as one could imagine. Although Shakespeare and his fellows prospered, their status under the law was conditional upon the protection of powerful patrons. "Common players"—those who did not have patrons or masters—were classed in the language of the law with "vagabonds and sturdy beggars." So the actors had to secure for themselves the official rank of servants of patrons. Among the patrons under whose protection Shakespeare's company worked were the lord chamberlain and, after the accession of King James in 1603, the king himself.

We are now perhaps on the verge of learning a great deal more about the theaters in which Shakespeare and his contemporaries performed—or at least of opening up new questions about them. Already about 70 percent of the Rose has been excavated, as has about 10 percent of the second Globe, the one built in 1614. It is to be hoped that soon more will be available for study. These are exciting times for students of Shakespeare's stage.

The Publication of Shakespeare's Plays

Eighteen of Shakespeare's plays found their way into print during the playwright's lifetime, but there is nothing to suggest that he took any interest in their publication. These eighteen appeared separately in editions called quartos. Their pages were not much larger than the one you are now reading, and these little books were sold unbound for a few pence. The earliest of the quartos that still survive were printed in 1594, the year that both *Titus Andronicus* and a version of the play now called *2 King Henry VI* became available. While almost every one of these early quartos displays on its title page the name of the acting company that performed the play, only about half provide the name of the playwright, Shakespeare. The first quarto edition to bear the name Shakespeare on its title page is *Love's Labor's Lost* of 1598. A few of these quartos were popular with the book-buying public of Shakespeare's lifetime; for example, quarto *Richard II* went through five editions between 1597 and 1615. But most of the quartos were far from best-sellers; *Love's Labor's Lost* (1598), for instance, was not reprinted in quarto until 1631. After Shakespeare's death, two more of his plays appeared in quarto format: *Othello* in 1622 and *The Two Noble Kinsmen*, coauthored with John Fletcher, in 1634.

In 1623, seven years after Shakespeare's death, *Mr. William Shakespeares Comedies, Histories, & Tragedies* was published. This printing offered readers in a single book thirty-six of the thirty-eight plays now thought to have been written by Shakespeare, including eighteen that had never been printed before. And it offered them in a style that was then reserved for serious literature and scholarship. The plays were arranged in double columns on pages nearly a foot high. This large page size is called "folio," as opposed to the smaller "quarto," and the 1623 volume is usually called the Shakespeare First Folio. It is reputed to have sold for the lordly price of a pound. (One copy at the Folger Library is marked fifteen shillings—that is, three-quarters of a pound.)

In a preface to the First Folio entitled "To the great Variety of Readers," two of Shakespeare's former fellow actors in the King's Men, John Heminge and Henry Condell, wrote that they themselves had collected their dead companion's plays. They suggested that they had seen his own papers: "we have scarce received from him a blot in his papers." The title page of the Folio declared that the plays within it had been printed "according to the True Original Copies." Comparing the Folio to the quartos, Heminge and Condell disparaged the quartos, advising their readers that "before you were abused with divers stolen and surreptitious copies, maimed, and deformed by the frauds and stealths of injurious impostors." Many Shakespeareans of the eighteenth and nineteenth centuries believed Heminge and Condell and regarded the Folio plays as superior to anything in the quartos.

Once we begin to examine the Folio plays in detail, it becomes less easy to take at face value the word of Heminge and Condell about the superiority of the Folio texts. For example, of the first nine plays in the Folio (one-quarter of the entire collection), four were essentially reprinted from earlier quarto printings that Heminge and Condell had disparaged; and four have now been identified as printed from copies written in the hand of a professional scribe of the 1620s named Ralph Crane; the ninth, *The Comedy of Errors,* was apparently also printed from a manuscript, but one whose origin cannot be readily identified. Evidently then, eight of the first nine plays in the First Folio were not printed, in spite of what the Folio title page announces, "according to the True Original Copies," or Shakespeare's own papers, and the source of the ninth is unknown. Since today's editors have been forced to treat Heminge and Condell's pronouncements with skepticism, they must choose whether to base their own editions upon quartos or the Folio on grounds other than Heminge and Condell's story of where the quarto and Folio versions originated.

Editors have often fashioned their own narratives to explain what lies behind the quartos and Folio. They have said that Heminge and Condell meant to criticize only a few of the early quartos, the ones that offer much shorter and sometimes quite different, often garbled, versions of plays. Among the examples of these are the 1600 quarto of *Henry V* (the Folio offers a much fuller version) or the 1603 *Hamlet* quarto (in 1604 a different, much longer form of the play got into print as a quarto). Early in this century editors speculated that these questionable texts were produced when someone in the audience took notes from the plays' dialogue during performances and then employed "hack poets" to fill out the notes. The poor results were then sold to a publisher and presented in print as Shakespeare's plays. More recently this story has given way to another in which the shorter versions are said to be re-creations from memory of Shakespeare's plays by actors who wanted to stage them in the provinces but lacked manuscript copies. Most of the quartos offer much better texts than these so-called bad quartos. Indeed, in most of the quartos we find texts that are at least equal to or better than what is printed in the Folio. Many of this century's Shakespeare enthusiasts have persuaded themselves that most of the quartos were set into type directly from Shakespeare's own papers, although there is nothing on which to base this conclusion except the desire for it to be true. Thus speculation continues about how the Shakespeare plays got to be printed. All that we have are the printed texts.

The book collector who was most successful in bringing together copies of the quartos and the First Folio was Henry Clay Folger, founder of the Folger Shakespeare Library in Washington, D.C. While it is estimated that there survive around the world only about 230 copies of the First Folio, Mr. Folger was able to acquire more than seventy-five copies, as well as a large number of fragments, for the library that bears his name. He also amassed a substantial number of quartos. For example, only fourteen copies of the First Quarto of *Love's Labor's Lost* are known to exist, and three are at the Folger Shakespeare Library. As a consequence of Mr. Folger's labors, twentieth-century scholars visiting the Folger Library have been able to learn a great deal about sixteenth- and seventeenth-century printing and, particularly, about the printing of Shakespeare's plays. And Mr. Folger did not stop at the First Folio, but collected many copies of later editions of Shakespeare, beginning with the Second Folio (1632), the Third (1663–64), and the Fourth (1685). Each of these later folios was based on its immediate predecessor and was edited anonymously. The first editor of Shakespeare whose name we know was Nicholas Rowe, whose first edition came out in 1709. Mr. Folger collected this edition and many, many more by Rowe's successors.

An Introduction to This Text

The Two Gentlemen of Verona was first printed in the 1623 collection of Shakespeare's plays now known as the First Folio. The present edition is based directly upon that printing.* For the convenience of the reader, we have modernized the punctuation and the spelling of the Folio. Sometimes we go so far as to modernize certain old forms of words; for example, usually when *a* means *he*, we change it to *he*; we change *mo* to *more*, and *ye* to *you*. But it is not our practice in editing any of the plays to modernize words that sound distinctly different from modern forms. For example, when the early printed texts read *sith* or *apricocks* or *porpentine*, we have not modernized to *since*, *apricots*, *porcupine*. When the forms *an*, *and*, or *and if* appear instead of the modern form *if*, we have reduced *and* to *an* but have not changed any of these forms to their modern equivalent, *if*. We also modernize and, where necessary, correct passages in foreign languages, unless an error in the early printed text can be reasonably explained as a joke.

Whenever we change the wording of the First Folio or add anything to its stage directions, we mark the change by enclosing it in superior half-brackets (⌐ ⌐). We want our readers to be immediately aware when we have intervened. (Only when we correct an obvious typographical error in the First Folio does the change not get marked.) Whenever we change either the First Folio's wording or its punctuation so that meaning changes, we

---

*We have also consulted the computerized text of the First Folio provided by the Text Archive of the Oxford University Computing Centre, to which we are grateful.

list the change in the textual notes at the back of the book, even if all we have done is fix an obvious error.

We regularize the spellings of a number of the proper names, as is becoming the usual practice in editions of the play. For example, for the Folio's spelling "Launce" we print "Lance"; for "Panthino," "Pantino"; for "Protheus," "Proteus"; for "Siluia," "Sylvia."

This edition differs from many earlier ones in its efforts to aid the reader in imagining the play as a performance rather than as a series of actual events. Thus, stage directions and speech prefixes are written with reference to the stage. For example, when one goes to a modern production of *Two Gentlemen of Verona*, one is always aware, after the actor playing Julia has donned her disguise, that she no longer looks like the gentlewoman that she first impersonated. Instead, the actor playing Julia looks like a page, and is given the name "Sebastian." In an effort to reproduce in our edition what an audience experiences, we have added her "disguise name" to the speech prefix JULIA whenever Julia is in dialogue with characters who address her as the page Sebastian. With the addition of such a direction to the speech prefix, we hope to help our readers stage the play in their own imaginations in a way that more closely approximates an experience in the theater.

For the same reason, whenever it is reasonably certain, in our view, that a speech is accompanied by a particular action, we provide a stage direction describing the action, setting the added direction in brackets to signal that it is not found in the Folio. (Occasional exceptions to this rule occur when the action is so obvious that to add a stage direction would insult the reader.) Stage directions for the entrance of a character in mid-scene are, with rare exceptions, placed so that they immediately precede the character's participation in the scene, even though these entrances may appear somewhat earlier in the early printed texts. In *Two Gentlemen of Verona*, we, like other editors of the play, are therefore required to intervene rather more strenuously than usual in placing stage directions. The First Folio text of *Two Gentlemen of Verona* lists at the beginning of each of its scenes all the characters who are to enter in the course of the scene, even though, in some cases, characters listed in a scene's opening entrance direction are not required onstage until many lines into the scene. Textual critics term such entrance directions as we find in *Two Gentlemen of Verona* "massed entries" and associate them with a particular scribe who is known to have copied out plays performed by Shakespeare's acting company. This scribe is called Ralph Crane, and many scholars believe that signs of his penmanship, including his characteristic spellings and lavish use of punctuation, are still legible in the First Folio's text of *Two Gentlemen of Verona*. Whenever we alter the position or content of stage directions, we record this change in the textual notes. Latin stage directions (e.g., *Exeunt*) are translated into English (e.g., *They exit*).

We expand the often severely abbreviated forms of names used as speech headings in early printed texts into the full names of the characters. We also regularize the speakers' names in speech headings, using only a single designation for each character, even though the early printed texts sometimes use a variety of designations. Variations in the speech headings of the early printed texts are recorded in the textual notes.

In the present edition, as well, we mark with a dash any change of address within a speech, unless a stage direction intervenes. When the *-ed* ending of a word is to be pronounced, we mark it with an accent. Like editors for the past two centuries, we print metrically linked lines in the following way:

SPEED
  Sir, your glove.
VALENTINE   Not mine. My gloves are on.
                            (2.1.1–2)

However, when there are a number of short verse-lines that can be linked in more than one way, we do not, with rare exceptions, indent any of them.

The Explanatory Notes

The notes that appear on the pages facing the text are designed to provide readers with the help that they may need to enjoy the play. Whenever the meaning of a word in the text is not readily accessible in a good contemporary dictionary, we offer the meaning in a note. Sometimes we provide a note even when the relevant meaning is to be found in the dictionary but when the word has acquired since Shakespeare's time other potentially confusing meanings. In our notes, we try to offer modern synonyms for Shakespeare's words. We also try to indicate to the reader the connection between the word in the play and the modern synonym. For example, Shakespeare sometimes uses the word *head* to mean *source*, but, for modern readers, there may be no connection evident between these two words. We provide the connection by explaining Shakespeare's usage as follows: "**head:** fountainhead, source." On some occasions, a whole phrase or clause needs explanation. Then we rephrase in our own words the difficult passage, and add at the end synonyms for individual words in the passage. When scholars have been unable to determine the meaning of a word or phrase, we acknowledge the uncertainty.

THE TWO
GENTLEMEN
OF VERONA

The names of all the Actors.

Duke : Father to Siluia.

Valentine. } the two Gentlemen.
Protheus. }

Anthonio: father to Protheus.

Thurio: a foolish riuall to Valentine.

Eglamoure : Agent for Siluia in her escape.

Host: where Iulia lodges.

Ous-lawes with Valentine.

Speed: a clownish seruant to Valentine.

Launce : the like to Protheus.

Panthion: seruant to Antonio.

Iulia: beloued of Protheus.

Siluia: beloued of Valentine.

Lucetta: waighting-woman to Iulia.

From the 1623 First Folio.
(Digitally rearranged from double columns to single column.)

Characters in the Play

VALENTINE, a gentleman of Verona
SPEED, his servant

PROTEUS, a gentleman of Verona
LANCE, his servant
ANTONIO, Proteus' father
PANTINO, an attendant to Antonio

JULIA, a lady of Verona
LUCETTA, her waiting-gentlewoman

SYLVIA, a lady of Milan
DUKE (sometimes Emperor), Sylvia's father

THURIO, a gentleman
EGLAMOUR, a gentleman

HOST, proprietor of an inn in Milan

OUTLAWS, living in a forest near Mantua

Servants; Musicians; Crab, a dog

THE TWO
GENTLEMEN
OF VERONA

ACT 1

1.1 Valentine, preparing to leave for Milan, says farewell to Proteus, who stays in Verona to be near Julia. Valentine's servant, Speed, informs Proteus that he has given Proteus' letter to Julia. Speed then leaves to join Valentine.

O SD. **Proteus:** The sea-god **Proteus** in Greek mythology could transform himself into any number of shapes; the name became equated with fickleness. It is here set in opposition to **Valentine,** a name associated with true love.

2. **Home-keeping:** i.e., stay-at-home; **homely:** simple, dull

3. **affection:** love

7. **sluggardized:** i.e., made lazy or sluggish

12. **haply:** by chance (Some editors argue that the Folio spelling, "hap'ly," means "happily," since it is not "by chance" that Valentine will be seeing **rare noteworthy** objects [line 13].)

15. **hap:** fortune

17. **Commend:** entrust, commit; **grievance:** suffering, pain

18. **beadsman:** i.e., one who prays for the soul of another (The word refers to the beads of the rosary.)

19. **love-book:** a book treating the subject of love (A **beadsman** would normally pray on a prayer book, not a **love-book.**)

ACT 1

Scene 1
⌜*Enter*⌝ *Valentine* ⌜*and*⌝ *Proteus.*

VALENTINE
Cease to persuade, my loving Proteus.
Home-keeping youth have ever homely wits.
Were 't not affection chains thy tender days
To the sweet glances of thy honored love,
I rather would entreat thy company   5
To see the wonders of the world abroad
Than, living dully sluggardized at home,
Wear out thy youth with shapeless idleness.
But since thou lov'st, love still and thrive therein,
Even as I would when I to love begin.   10

PROTEUS
Wilt thou be gone? Sweet Valentine, adieu.
Think on thy Proteus when thou haply seest
Some rare noteworthy object in thy travel.
Wish me partaker in thy happiness
When thou dost meet good hap; and in thy danger,   15
If ever danger do environ thee,
Commend thy grievance to my holy prayers,
For I will be thy beadsman, Valentine.

VALENTINE
And on a love-book pray for my success?

PROTEUS
Upon some book I love I'll pray for thee.   20

7

22. **Leander:** a famous lover in Greek mythology who drowned while trying to reach his love by swimming across the **Hellespont** (See page 18.)

24. **over shoes:** deeply immersed (with wordplay on "over-shoes," i.e., up to the ankles)

25. **over boots in:** i.e., recklessly committed to pursuing

27. **give me not the boots:** proverbial (meaning, perhaps, don't make a fool of me) There may also be a reference here to **the boots,** a Scottish instrument of torture used to extort confessions from prisoners. (See page 116.)

28. **boots:** profits

33. **watchful:** wakeful

35. **If lost . . . labor won:** i.e., if the object of one's love is **lost,** then all one has gained is **a grievous labor**

36. **How ever:** i.e., in either case; **but:** merely; **wit:** mind, intellect

38. **circumstance:** circumlocution

39. **circumstance:** situation, condition

40. **love, Love:** Here, as elsewhere in the play, the meaning shifts between **love** as an emotion or passion and love's personification as **Love,** i.e., Cupid, the Roman god of love. (See page 66.) It is not always clear which meaning is intended.

42. **yokèd:** subjugated, enslaved

43. **Methinks:** i.e., it seems to me; **chronicled for:** put on record as

VALENTINE

    That's on some shallow story of deep love,

    How young Leander crossed the Hellespont.

PROTEUS

    That's a deep story of a deeper love,

    For he was more than over shoes in love.

VALENTINE

    'Tis true, for you are over boots in love,   25

    And yet you never swam the Hellespont.

PROTEUS

    Over the boots? Nay, give me not the boots.

VALENTINE

    No, I will not, for it boots thee not.

PROTEUS   What?

VALENTINE

    To be in love, where scorn is bought with groans,   30

    Coy looks with heart-sore sighs, one fading

        moment's mirth

    With twenty watchful, weary, tedious nights;

    If haply won, perhaps a hapless gain;

    If lost, why then a grievous labor won;   35

    How ever, but a folly bought with wit,

    Or else a wit by folly vanquishèd.

PROTEUS

    So, by your circumstance, you call me fool.

VALENTINE

    So, by your circumstance, I fear you'll prove.

PROTEUS

    'Tis love you cavil at; I am not Love.   40

VALENTINE

    Love is your master, for he masters you;

    And he that is so yokèd by a fool

    Methinks should not be chronicled for wise.

PROTEUS

    Yet writers say: as in the sweetest bud

45. **canker:** cankerworm, grub (See below.)
46. **Inhabits:** dwells
47. **most forward:** earliest
48. **blow:** blossoms
50. **blasting:** blighted
51. **his:** i.e., its; **the prime:** springtime (for the lover, the springtime of his life)
53. **wherefore:** why
54. **fond:** foolish
55. **road:** i.e., harbor
56. **shipped:** embarked, aboard the ship
58. **take our leave:** bid farewell (to each other)
59. **Milan:** pronounced "mìllin" (as in the word "millinery") See page xvi.
60. **success:** fortunes (good or bad)
66. **friends:** This word often meant "relatives, family," and probably does so here.

A cankerworm. (1.1.45, 48)
From John Johnstone, [*Opera aliquot,*] (1650–62).

The eating canker dwells, so eating love   45
Inhabits in the finest wits of all.

VALENTINE
And writers say: as the most forward bud
Is eaten by the canker ere it blow,
Even so by love the young and tender wit
Is turned to folly, blasting in the bud,   50
Losing his verdure, even in the prime,
And all the fair effects of future hopes.
But wherefore waste I time to counsel thee
That art a votary to fond desire?
Once more adieu. My father at the road   55
Expects my coming, there to see me shipped.

PROTEUS
And thither will I bring thee, Valentine.

VALENTINE
Sweet Proteus, no. Now let us take our leave.
To Milan let me hear from thee by letters
Of thy success in love, and what news else   60
Betideth here in absence of thy friend.
And I likewise will visit thee with mine.

PROTEUS
All happiness bechance to thee in Milan.

VALENTINE
As much to you at home. And so farewell.   *He exits.*

PROTEUS
He after honor hunts, I after love.   65
He leaves his friends, to dignify them more;
I ⌜leave⌝ myself, my friends, and all, for love.
Thou, Julia, thou hast metamorphosed me,
Made me neglect my studies, lose my time,
War with good counsel, set the world at nought;   70
Made wit with musing weak, heart sick with thought.

⌜*Enter*⌝ *Speed.*

72. **'save you:** i.e., God save you (a conventional greeting)

73. **But now:** only this moment, just now

75. **sheep:** stupid person (punning on the sound of "ship" in the word **shipped**)

77. **An if:** i.e., if

81–82. **my horns . . . wake or sleep:** probably an allusion to the nursery rhyme "Little Boy Blue" (See longer note, page 189, and picture, page 172.)

86. **circumstance:** particular case or instance

87. **It shall . . . but I'll:** i.e., I'm sure that I'll be able to

95. **cry "baa":** i.e., bleat like a sheep (with a possible pun on "bah," an expression of impatient rejection or contempt)

98. **mutton:** i.e., sheep

99. **laced mutton:** a phrase usually describing a courtesan, but sometimes indicating merely a richly dressed woman (See longer note, page 190.)

SPEED
  Sir Proteus, 'save you. Saw you my master?
PROTEUS
  But now he parted hence to embark for Milan.
SPEED
  Twenty to one, then, he is shipped already,
  And I have played the sheep in losing him.   75
PROTEUS
  Indeed a sheep doth very often stray,
  An if the shepherd be awhile away.
SPEED   You conclude that my master is a shepherd,
  then, and I ⌜a⌝ sheep?
PROTEUS   I do.   80
SPEED   Why, then my horns are his horns, whether I
  wake or sleep.
PROTEUS   A silly answer, and fitting well a sheep.
SPEED   This proves me still a sheep.
PROTEUS   True, and thy master a shepherd.   85
SPEED   Nay, that I can deny by a circumstance.
PROTEUS   It shall go hard but I'll prove it by another.
SPEED   The shepherd seeks the sheep, and not the
  sheep the shepherd; but I seek my master, and my
  master seeks not me. Therefore I am no sheep.   90
PROTEUS   The sheep for fodder follow the shepherd; the
  shepherd for food follows not the sheep. Thou for
  wages followest thy master; thy master for wages
  follows not thee. Therefore thou art a sheep.
SPEED   Such another proof will make me cry "baa."   95
PROTEUS   But dost thou hear? Gav'st thou my letter to
  Julia?
SPEED   Ay, sir. I, a lost mutton, gave your letter to her, a
  laced mutton, and she, a laced mutton, gave me, a
  lost mutton, nothing for my labor.   100
PROTEUS   Here's too small a pasture for such store of
  muttons.

103. **overcharged:** too crowded

104. **stick:** stab, kill (with a probable bawdy double meaning)

105. **pound:** (1) enclose in a pound; (2) crush by beating (Speed responds as if the word meant the sum of money he was to receive.)

110. **a pin:** i.e., a worthless object

115. **noddy:** fool, simpleton

120. **take it for your pains:** an expression used when offering a gratuity (as in lines 132–33 and 145)

122. **fain:** obliged, content; **bear with:** put up with

124. **Marry:** i.e., indeed (originally, an oath on the name of the Virgin Mary); **orderly:** properly, duly

126. **Beshrew me:** a mild oath (originally meaning "curse me")

128. **open:** reveal, disclose

136. **perceive:** comprehend, understand (but used by Speed, line 138, in its meaning of "obtain, receive")

SPEED If the ground be overcharged, you were best
  stick her.

PROTEUS Nay, in that you are astray; 'twere best pound 105
  you.

SPEED Nay, sir, less than a pound shall serve me for
  carrying your letter.

PROTEUS You mistake; I mean the pound, a pinfold.

SPEED
  From a pound to a pin? Fold it over and over, 110
  'Tis threefold too little for carrying a letter to your
  lover.

PROTEUS But what said she?

SPEED, ⌜*nodding*⌝ Ay.

PROTEUS Nod—"Ay." Why, that's "noddy." 115

SPEED You mistook, sir. I say she did nod, and you ask
  me if she did nod, and I say "ay."

PROTEUS And that set together is "noddy."

SPEED Now you have taken the pains to set it together,
  take it for your pains. 120

PROTEUS No, no, you shall have it for bearing the letter.

SPEED Well, I perceive I must be fain to bear with you.

PROTEUS Why, sir, how do you bear with me?

SPEED Marry, sir, the letter, very orderly, having nothing but the word "noddy" for my pains. 125

PROTEUS Beshrew me, but you have a quick wit.

SPEED And yet it cannot overtake your slow purse.

PROTEUS Come, come, open the matter in brief. What
  said she?

SPEED Open your purse, that the money and the matter 130
  may be both at once delivered.

PROTEUS, ⌜*giving money*⌝ Well, sir, here is for your
  pains. What said she?

SPEED, ⌜*looking at the money*⌝ Truly, sir, I think you'll
  hardly win her. 135

PROTEUS Why? Couldst thou perceive so much from
  her?

139. **ducat:** gold coin

141. **in telling:** i.e., when you tell her

147. **testerned me:** i.e., given me a tester (a slang term for a sixpence)

148–49. **commend you to:** i.e., give your greetings to

150. **wrack:** shipwreck (Proverbial: "He that is born to be hanged shall never be drowned.")

154. **deign:** graciously accept

155. **post:** messenger; ignorant dolt

1.2 Julia receives Proteus' letter and pretends to be very angry at his presumption.

———

4. **resort:** gathering

5. **parle:** conversation

6. **worthiest:** i.e., most deserving of

SPEED   Sir, I could perceive nothing at all from her, no,
        not so much as a ducat for delivering your letter.
        And being so hard to me that brought your mind, I   140
        fear she'll prove as hard to you in telling your mind.
        Give her no token but stones, for she's as hard as
        steel.

PROTEUS   What said she? Nothing?

SPEED   No, not so much as "Take this for thy pains."   145
        To testify your bounty, I thank you, you have
        ⌜testerned⌝ me. In requital whereof, henceforth
        carry your letters yourself. And so, sir, I'll com-
        mend you to my master.

PROTEUS
    Go, go, begone, to save your ship from wrack,   150
    Which cannot perish having thee aboard,
    Being destined to a drier death on shore.
                                     ⌜*Speed exits.*⌝
    I must go send some better messenger.
    I fear my Julia would not deign my lines,
    Receiving them from such a worthless post.   155
                                     He exits.

                        Scene 2
                Enter Julia and Lucetta.

JULIA
    But say, Lucetta, now we are alone,
    Wouldst thou then counsel me to fall in love?

LUCETTA
    Ay, madam, so you stumble not unheedfully.

JULIA
    Of all the fair resort of gentlemen
    That every day with parle encounter me,   5
    In thy opinion which is worthiest love?

14. **gentle:** wellborn, courteous
17. **passing:** i.e., surpassing
19. **censure . . . on:** give an opinion . . . of; **lovely:** loving, amorous
23. **woman's reason:** Proverbial: " 'Because' is woman's reason."
27. **moved:** i.e., made a proposal or request to

Leander swimming the Hellespont. (1.1.22, 3.1.119)
From Grammaticus Musaeus, [*Hero and Leander,*] (1538).

LUCETTA
  Please you repeat their names, I'll show my mind
  According to my shallow simple skill.

JULIA
  What think'st thou of the fair Sir Eglamour?

LUCETTA
  As of a knight well-spoken, neat, and fine;   10
  But, were I you, he never should be mine.

JULIA
  What think'st thou of the rich Mercatio?

LUCETTA
  Well of his wealth, but of himself so-so.

JULIA
  What think'st thou of the gentle Proteus?

LUCETTA
  Lord, Lord, to see what folly reigns in us!   15

JULIA
  How now? What means this passion at his name?

LUCETTA
  Pardon, dear madam, 'tis a passing shame
  That I, unworthy body as I am,
  Should censure thus on lovely gentlemen.

JULIA
  Why not on Proteus, as of all the rest?   20

LUCETTA
  Then thus: of many good, I think him best.

JULIA Your reason?

LUCETTA
  I have no other but a woman's reason:
  I think him so because I think him so.

JULIA
  And wouldst thou have me cast my love on him?   25

LUCETTA
  Ay, if you thought your love not cast away.

JULIA
  Why, he of all the rest hath never moved me

30. **closest:** i.e., most tightly confined
43. **goodly broker:** i.e., proper or convenient go-between
44. **wanton:** amorous
46. **office:** service, duty; position of responsibility
47. **officer:** one who performs a duty; agent
52. **That:** i.e., so that
53. **I would:** i.e., I wish; **o'erlooked:** read

LUCETTA
  Yet he of all the rest I think best loves you.
JULIA
  His little speaking shows his love but small.
LUCETTA
  Fire that's closest kept burns most of all.   30
JULIA
  They do not love that do not show their love.
LUCETTA
  O, they love least that let men know their love.
JULIA   I would I knew his mind.
LUCETTA, ⌐*handing her a paper*¬ Peruse this paper,
    madam.   35
JULIA ⌐*reads*¬ "To Julia."—Say from whom.
LUCETTA   That the contents will show.
JULIA   Say, say who gave it thee.
LUCETTA
  Sir Valentine's page; and sent, I think, from
    Proteus.   40
  He would have given it you, but I, being in the way,
  Did in your name receive it. Pardon the fault, I pray.
JULIA
  Now, by my modesty, a goodly broker!
  Dare you presume to harbor wanton lines?
  To whisper and conspire against my youth?   45
  Now trust me, 'tis an office of great worth,
  And you an officer fit for the place.
  There, take the paper; see it be returned,
  Or else return no more into my sight.
LUCETTA, ⌐*taking the paper*¬
  To plead for love deserves more fee than hate.   50
JULIA
  Will you be gone?
LUCETTA   That you may ruminate. *She exits*.
JULIA
  And yet I would I had o'erlooked the letter.

54. **It were a shame:** i.e., it would be disgraceful

55. **to a fault:** i.e., to commit an offense

56. **What fool is she:** i.e., what a fool she is; **maid:** maiden, unmarried girl

62. **presently:** soon, immediately; **kiss the rod:** proverbial for "accept punishment meekly"

65. **angerly:** angrily

68. **remission:** pardon

73. **kill your stomach:** (1) suppress your appetite; (2) destroy your anger; **meat:** food

74. **maid:** maidservant

It were a shame to call her back again
And pray her to a fault for which I chid her.   55
What fool is she that knows I am a maid
And would not force the letter to my view,
Since maids in modesty say "no" to that
Which they would have the profferer construe "ay"!
Fie, fie, how wayward is this foolish love   60
That like a testy babe will scratch the nurse
And presently, all humbled, kiss the rod!
How churlishly I chid Lucetta hence,
When willingly I would have had her here!
How angerly I taught my brow to frown,   65
When inward joy enforced my heart to smile!
My penance is to call Lucetta back
And ask remission for my folly past.—
What ho, Lucetta!

⌐*Enter Lucetta.*⌐

LUCETTA   What would your Ladyship?   70
JULIA
  Is 't near dinner time?
LUCETTA   I would it were,
  That you might kill your stomach on your meat
  And not upon your maid.
                  ⌐*She drops a paper and then retrieves it.*⌐
JULIA
  What is 't that you took up so gingerly?   75
LUCETTA Nothing.
JULIA Why didst thou stoop, then?
LUCETTA
  To take a paper up that I let fall.
JULIA And is that paper nothing?
LUCETTA Nothing concerning me.   80
JULIA
  Then let it lie for those that it concerns.

82. **lie where it concerns:** i.e., speak untruthfully in matters of importance

85. **That:** i.e., in order that

86. **set:** i.e., compose a tune (The words **tune, note,** and **set** begin a series of puns on musical terms that continues through line 103 with the words **burden, sharp, flat, concord, descant, mean,** and **bass**.)

87. **As little:** i.e., **set as little** ("To set little by" meant "to have low regard for.") **toys:** trifles

88. **"Light o' Love":** the name of a song referred to by Shakespeare in other plays as well

89. **heavy:** serious, important

90. **Belike:** no doubt, probably; **burden:** (1) load; (2) bass accompaniment

93. **reach so high:** (1) i.e., sing such **high** notes; (2) i.e., love someone so much above my social rank

94. **minion:** a term of contempt

95. **tune:** (1) proper pitch; (2) mood, temper

98. **sharp:** i.e., raised in pitch a semitone, or above the proper pitch (perhaps a pun involving stage action) See longer note, page 190.

99. **saucy:** insolent

100. **flat:** plain, blunt (with wordplay on the musical sense)

101. **descant:** an ornamental melody sung above a musical theme

102. **There . . . mean:** i.e., there is lacking only a middle or tenor part ("Trebles and basses make poor music without means" [*The Atheist's Tragedy*, 3.3 (1611)].)

104. **bid the base:** a term from a game called "prisoner's base" (Editors disagree about the meaning of the term in this context.)

LUCETTA
    Madam, it will not lie where it concerns
    Unless it have a false interpreter.

JULIA
    Some love of yours hath writ to you in rhyme.

LUCETTA
    That I might sing it, madam, to a tune,   85
    Give me a note. Your Ladyship can set—

JULIA
    As little by such toys as may be possible.
    Best sing it to the tune of "Light o' Love."

LUCETTA
    It is too heavy for so light a tune.

JULIA
    Heavy? Belike it hath some burden then?   90

LUCETTA
    Ay, and melodious were it, would you sing it.

JULIA
    And why not you?

LUCETTA   I cannot reach so high.

JULIA, ⌜*taking the paper*⌝
    Let's see your song. How now, minion!

LUCETTA
    Keep tune there still, so you will sing it out.   95
    And yet methinks I do not like this tune.

JULIA   You do not?

LUCETTA   No, madam, 'tis too sharp.

JULIA   You, minion, are too saucy.

LUCETTA   Nay, now you are too flat   100
    And mar the concord with too harsh a descant.
    There wanteth but a mean to fill your song.

JULIA
    The mean is drowned with ⌜your⌝ unruly bass.

LUCETTA
    Indeed, I bid the base for Proteus.

106. **coil:** disturbance, fuss

109. **makes it strange:** i.e., pretends to be indignant (The phrase could also mean "keeps a standoffish attitude.")

115. **several paper:** separate piece of **paper**

118. **thy name:** i.e., a piece of paper on which is written the word **Julia**

122. **throughly:** thoroughly

123. **search it:** i.e., probe the **wound** (medical language, continued in **sovereign**, used to describe remedies that are extremely potent)

127. **That . . . bear:** i.e., let **some whirlwind** carry **that**

133. **sith:** since

"Injurious wasps, to feed on such
sweet honey . . ." (1.2.113)
From Henry Peacham, *Minerua Britanna* . . . [1612].

JULIA
>This babble shall not henceforth trouble me.   105
>Here is a coil with protestation.
>>⌐She rips up the paper. Lucetta begins
>>   to pick up the pieces.⌐
>Go, get you gone, and let the papers lie.
>You would be fing'ring them to anger me.

LUCETTA
>She makes it strange, but she would be best pleased
>To be so angered with another letter.   ⌐She exits.⌐ 110

JULIA
>Nay, would I were so angered with the same!
>O hateful hands, to tear such loving words!
>Injurious wasps, to feed on such sweet honey
>And kill the bees that yield it with your stings!
>I'll kiss each several paper for amends.   115
>>⌐She picks up some pieces.⌐
>Look, here is writ "kind Julia." Unkind Julia,
>As in revenge of thy ingratitude,
>I throw thy name against the bruising stones,
>Trampling contemptuously on thy disdain.
>And here is writ "love-wounded Proteus."   120
>Poor wounded name, my bosom as a bed
>Shall lodge thee till thy wound be throughly healed,
>And thus I search it with a sovereign kiss.
>But twice or thrice was "Proteus" written down.
>Be calm, good wind. Blow not a word away   125
>Till I have found each letter in the letter
>Except mine own name. That some whirlwind bear
>Unto a ragged, fearful, hanging rock
>And throw it thence into the raging sea.
>Lo, here in one line is his name twice writ: 130
>"Poor forlorn Proteus, passionate Proteus,
>To the sweet Julia." That I'll tear away—
>And yet I will not, sith so prettily
>He couples it to his complaining names.

137. **stays:** waits

140. **respect:** value, prize; **best . . . up:** i.e., it would be **best** to pick them up

141. **taken up:** reprimanded sharply

142. **for catching:** i.e., lest they should catch

143. **month's mind:** liking, fancy

145. **judge I wink:** suppose that my eyes are closed

1.3 Proteus, reading a letter from Julia, encounters his father, Antonio, and tells him that the letter is from Valentine, who wishes Proteus were with him in Milan. Antonio informs Proteus that he is to leave immediately to join Valentine in Milan.

———————

1. **sad:** serious

2. **Wherewith:** with which

6. **suffer:** allow

Thus will I fold them one upon another.   135
Now kiss, embrace, contend, do what you will.

⌜*Enter Lucetta.*⌝

LUCETTA
Madam, dinner is ready, and your father stays.
JULIA   Well, let us go.
LUCETTA
What, shall these papers lie like telltales here?
JULIA
If you respect them, best to take them up.   140
LUCETTA
Nay, I was taken up for laying them down.
Yet here they shall not lie, for catching cold.
              ⌜*She picks up the rest of the pieces.*⌝
JULIA
I see you have a month's mind to them.
LUCETTA
Ay, madam, you may say what sights you see;
I see things too, although you judge I wink.   145
JULIA   Come, come, will 't please you go?
                              They exit.

Scene 3
Enter Antonio and Pantino.

ANTONIO
Tell me, Pantino, what sad talk was that
Wherewith my brother held you in the cloister?
PANTINO
'Twas of his nephew Proteus, your son.
ANTONIO
Why, what of him?
PANTINO   He wondered that your Lordship   5
Would suffer him to spend his youth at home

8. **preferment:** advancement in condition, status, or position in life

13. **meet:** fit, proper

16. **impeachment:** detriment; discredit, disparagement

19. **hammering:** earnestly deliberating

21. **perfect:** thoroughly accomplished

24. **perfected:** accent on first syllable

28. **Emperor:** See longer note, page 190.

30. **him:** i.e., Proteus

31. **tilts and tournaments:** medieval sports that even in the sixteenth century were part of the essential education of young noblemen (See pages xxxvi–xxxvii.)

33. **in eye of:** i.e., able to see

While other men, of slender reputation,
Put forth their sons to seek preferment out:
Some to the wars to try their fortune there,
Some to discover islands far away, 10
Some to the studious universities.
For any or for all these exercises
He said that Proteus your son was meet,
And did request me to importune you
To let him spend his time no more at home, 15
Which would be great impeachment to his age
In having known no travel in his youth.

ANTONIO
Nor need'st thou much importune me to that
Whereon this month I have been hammering.
I have considered well his loss of time 20
And how he cannot be a perfect man,
Not being tried and tutored in the world.
Experience is by industry achieved
And perfected by the swift course of time.
Then tell me whither were I best to send him. 25

PANTINO
I think your Lordship is not ignorant
How his companion, youthful Valentine,
Attends the Emperor in his royal court.

ANTONIO I know it well.

PANTINO
'Twere good, I think, your Lordship sent him thither. 30
There shall he practice tilts and tournaments,
Hear sweet discourse, converse with noblemen,
And be in eye of every exercise
Worthy his youth and nobleness of birth.

ANTONIO
I like thy counsel. Well hast thou advised, 35
And that thou mayst perceive how well I like it,
The execution of it shall make known.

40. **may . . . you:** a deferential phrase of address

45. **in good time:** just at the right moment; **break with him:** reveal to him what's in our minds

46. **lines:** i.e., words, writing

47. **hand:** handwriting

53. **May 't . . . Lordship:** a deferential phrase of address

54. **commendations:** greetings

59. **gracèd:** shown favor to

61. **stand you affected:** i.e., are you disposed

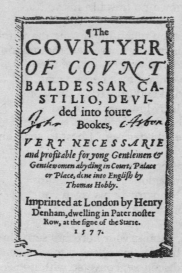

¶ The
COVRTYER
OF COVNT
BALDESSAR CA-
STILIO, DEVI-
ded into foure
Bookes,

VERY NECESSARIE
and profitable for yong Gentlemen &
Gentlewomen abyding in Court, Palace
or Place, done into English by
Thomas Hobby.

Imprinted at London by Henry
Denham, dwelling in Pater noster
Row, at the signe of the Starre.
1577.

The title page of the most famous Renaissance handbook
for fashioning the ideal gentleman.
From Baldassare Castiglione, *The Courtier* (1577).

Even with the speediest expedition
I will dispatch him to the Emperor's court.

PANTINO
Tomorrow, may it please you, Don Alphonso,   40
With other gentlemen of good esteem,
Are journeying to salute the Emperor
And to commend their service to his will.

ANTONIO
Good company. With them shall Proteus go.

⌈*Enter*⌉ *Proteus* ⌈*reading.*⌉

And in good time! Now will we break with him.   45

PROTEUS, ⌈*to himself*⌉
Sweet love, sweet lines, sweet life!
Here is her hand, the agent of her heart;
Here is her oath for love, her honor's pawn.
O, that our fathers would applaud our loves
To seal our happiness with their consents.   50
O heavenly Julia!

ANTONIO
How now? What letter are you reading there?

PROTEUS
May 't please your Lordship, 'tis a word or two
Of commendations sent from Valentine,
Delivered by a friend that came from him.   55

ANTONIO
Lend me the letter. Let me see what news.

PROTEUS
There is no news, my lord, but that he writes
How happily he lives, how well beloved
And daily gracèd by the Emperor,
Wishing me with him, partner of his fortune.   60

ANTONIO
And how stand you affected to his wish?

64. **something sorted:** i.e., somewhat in agreement

65. **Muse:** wonder

66. **there an end:** i.e., there's no more to say

69. **friends:** family

70. **Like exhibition:** i.e., the same support

72. **Excuse it not:** make no excuses; **peremptory:** resolved

75. **Look what thou want'st:** Whatever you need

76. **stay:** delay, postponement, waiting

78. **expedition:** journey

82. **take exceptions to:** object to

83. **vantage:** benefit

84. **excepted most against:** i.e., done the most damage to (literally, objected most to)

PROTEUS
  As one relying on your Lordship's will,
  And not depending on his friendly wish.

ANTONIO
  My will is something sorted with his wish.
  Muse not that I thus suddenly proceed,   65
  For what I will, I will, and there an end.
  I am resolved that thou shalt spend some time
  With Valentinus in the Emperor's court.
  What maintenance he from his friends receives,
  Like exhibition thou shalt have from me.   70
  Tomorrow be in readiness to go.
  Excuse it not, for I am peremptory.

PROTEUS
  My lord, I cannot be so soon provided.
  Please you deliberate a day or two

ANTONIO
  Look what thou want'st shall be sent after thee.   75
  No more of stay. Tomorrow thou must go.—
  Come on, Pantino; you shall be employed
  To hasten on his expedition.
                        ⌜*Antonio and Pantino exit.*⌝

PROTEUS
  Thus have I shunned the fire for fear of burning
  And drenched me in the sea, where I am drowned.   80
  I feared to show my father Julia's letter
  Lest he should take exceptions to my love,
  And with the vantage of mine own excuse
  Hath he excepted most against my love.
  O, how this spring of love resembleth   85
  The uncertain glory of an April day,
  Which now shows all the beauty of the sun,
  And by and by a cloud takes all away.

                ⌜*Enter Pantino.*⌝

91. **accords:** assents, consents

Friendship.
From Richard Brathwait, *The English gentleman . . .* (1633).

PANTINO
 Sir Proteus, your ⌜father⌝ calls for you.
 He is in haste. Therefore, I pray you, go.   90
PROTEUS
 Why, this it is: my heart accords thereto.
 ⌜*Aside.*⌝ And yet a thousand times it answers "no."
              They exit.

THE TWO
GENTLEMEN
OF VERONA

ACT 2

2.1 Valentine learns (with Speed's help) that the letter Sylvia had him write conveying her love to an admirer was intended for himself.

---

3. **one: On** and **one** were obviously pronounced much the same, since there were many such puns on the two words.

8. **How now:** an interjection (elliptical for "how is it now"); **sirrah:** a form of address to a male social inferior

12. **you'll still be:** i.e., you are always

14. **Go to:** an expression of impatience

18. **Marry:** i.e., indeed (originally an oath on the name of the Virgin Mary)

20. **relish:** sing, warble

"To wreathe your arms . . ." (2.1.19)
From [Robert Burton,] *The anatomy of melancholy . . .* (1638).

ACT 2

Scene 1
Enter Valentine ⌈and⌉ Speed, ⌈carrying a glove.⌉

SPEED
  Sir, your glove.
VALENTINE   Not mine. My gloves are on.
SPEED
  Why, then, this may be yours, for this is but one.
VALENTINE
  Ha? Let me see. Ay, give it me, it's mine.
  Sweet ornament that decks a thing divine!   5
  Ah, Sylvia, Sylvia!
SPEED, ⌈*calling*⌉ Madam Sylvia! Madam Sylvia!
VALENTINE How now, sirrah?
SPEED She is not within hearing, sir.
VALENTINE Why, sir, who bade you call her?   10
SPEED Your Worship, sir, or else I mistook.
VALENTINE Well, you'll still be too forward.
SPEED And yet I was last chidden for being too slow.
VALENTINE Go to, sir. Tell me, do you know Madam
    Sylvia?   15
SPEED She that your Worship loves?
VALENTINE Why, how know you that I am in love?
SPEED Marry, by these special marks: first, you have
    learned, like Sir Proteus, to wreathe your arms like
    a malcontent; to relish a love song like a robin   20
    redbreast; to walk alone like one that had the

41

23. **ABC:** spelling book, primer

24. **grandam:** grandmother; **takes diet:** i.e., is on a diet (from the French *observer une diète*)

25. **watch:** stay awake; **puling:** plaintively

26. **at Hallowmas:** i.e., on All Saints' Day (There is some evidence that beggars asked special alms on this day.)

29. **presently:** immediately; **sadly:** i.e., sad, serious

30. **want:** lack

31. **with:** i.e., by; **that:** i.e., so that

34. **without you:** i.e., in your appearance and behavior (literally, "on your exterior") Usually **without you** would mean "in your absence," and this is the sense the phrase seems to have in Valentine's reply (line 35).

36–37. **without you were:** i.e., if you were not

37. **would:** i.e., **would** perceive them

37–38. **so without:** i.e., so much on the outside of (i.e., surrounding)

40. **urinal:** a glass vessel employed to hold urine for medical examination; **not . . . but:** i.e., every **eye that sees you**

49. **hard-favored:** ugly

50. **fair:** beautiful; **well-favored:** (1) handsome; (2) filled with grace and exceptional kindness

53. **of you, well-favored:** i.e., looked on by you with approval

55. **favor:** grace and kindness (In the next line, Speed plays on the sense of **favor** as "face.")

pestilence; to sigh like a schoolboy that had lost his
ABC; to weep like a young wench that had buried
her grandam; to fast like one that takes diet; to
watch like one that fears robbing; to speak puling 25
like a beggar at Hallowmas. You were wont, when
you laughed, to crow like a cock; when you walked,
to walk like one of the lions. When you fasted, it was
presently after dinner; when you looked sadly, it
was for want of money. And now you are metamor- 30
phosed with a mistress, that when I look on you, I
can hardly think you my master.

VALENTINE Are all these things perceived in me?

SPEED They are all perceived without you.

VALENTINE Without me? They cannot. 35

SPEED Without you? Nay, that's certain, for without
you were so simple, none else would. But you are so
without these follies, that these follies are within
you and shine through you like the water in an
urinal, that not an eye that sees you but is a 40
physician to comment on your malady.

VALENTINE But tell me, dost thou know my Lady
Sylvia?

SPEED She that you gaze on so as she sits at supper?

VALENTINE Hast thou observed that? Even she I mean. 45

SPEED Why, sir, I know her not.

VALENTINE Dost thou know her by my gazing on her
and yet know'st her not?

SPEED Is she not hard-favored, sir?

VALENTINE Not so fair, boy, as well-favored. 50

SPEED Sir, I know that well enough.

VALENTINE What dost thou know?

SPEED That she is not so fair as, of you, well-favored.

VALENTINE I mean that her beauty is exquisite but her
favor infinite. 53

57. **out of all count:** incalculable

60. **counts of:** thinks much of, values

61. **How esteem'st thou me:** i.e., what estimation do you hold me in; **account of:** think highly of

70. **love is blind:** proverbial ("Love looks not with the eyes but with the mind; / And therefore is winged Cupid painted blind" [*A Midsummer Night's Dream* 1.1.240–41].) See below and page 66.

71. **lights:** ability to see; sight

72–73. **going ungartered:** i.e., forgetting to tie his hose with a garter

75. **passing:** surpassing, great

79. **Belike:** perhaps, probably

82. **swinged:** beat, thrashed

84. **stand affected to:** remain in love with

85. **would:** wish; **set:** seated (rather than standing)

"Love is blind." (2.1.70)
From an anonymous engraving inserted in Jacques Callot, *La petite passion* [n.d.].

SPEED   That's because the one is painted, and the other
    out of all count.

VALENTINE   How painted? And how out of count?

SPEED   Marry, sir, so painted to make her fair, that no
    man counts of her beauty.   60

VALENTINE   How esteem'st thou me? I account of her
    beauty.

SPEED   You never saw her since she was deformed.

VALENTINE   How long hath she been deformed?

SPEED   Ever since you loved her.   65

VALENTINE   I have loved her ever since I saw her, and
    still I see her beautiful.

SPEED   If you love her, you cannot see her.

VALENTINE   Why?

SPEED   Because love is blind. O, that you had mine eyes,   70
    or your own eyes had the lights they were wont to
    have when you chid at Sir Proteus for going ungar-
    tered!

VALENTINE   What should I see then?

SPEED   Your own present folly and her passing deformi-   75
    ty; for he, being in love, could not see to garter his
    hose, and you, being in love, cannot see to put on
    your hose.

VALENTINE   Belike, boy, then you are in love, for last
    morning you could not see to wipe my shoes.   80

SPEED   True, sir, I was in love with my bed. I thank you,
    you swinged me for my love, which makes me the
    bolder to chide you for yours.

VALENTINE   In conclusion, I stand affected to her.

SPEED   I would you were set, so your affection would   85
    cease.

VALENTINE   Last night she enjoined me to write some
    lines to one she loves.

SPEED   And have you?

VALENTINE   I have.   90

94. **motion:** puppet show (Speed sees Sylvia as the **puppet** and Valentine as the interpreter who will provide the dialogue.)

95. **to her:** i.e., for her

96–97. **good-morrows:** good-mornings

98. **give ye good ev'n:** i.e., God give you good even (a salutation used anytime after noon)

100. **servant:** one devoted to the service of a lady

102. **interest:** wordplay on Valentine's **interest** in Sylvia and her giving him **interest,** in the financial sense, on his **thousand good-morrows**

108. **clerkly:** learnedly, skillfully

109. **it came hardly off:** i.e., it was hard for me to write it

111. **doubtfully:** uncertainly, hesitatingly

113. **So it stead:** i.e., if it helps

114. **Please you:** i.e., if it please you to (a deferential phrase)

116. **A pretty period:** i.e., a nice conclusion (Sylvia's ironic comment on Valentine's **"And yet,"** a phrase that she repeats with various "sequels" in lines 117–19)

SPEED   Are they not lamely writ?

VALENTINE   No, boy, but as well as I can do them.
Peace, here she comes.

⌐*Enter*⌐ *Sylvia.*

SPEED, ⌐*aside*⌐   O excellent motion! O exceeding puppet! Now will he interpret to her.   95

VALENTINE   Madam and mistress, a thousand good-
morrows.

SPEED, ⌐*aside*⌐   O, give ye good ev'n! Here's a million of
manners.

SYLVIA   Sir Valentine, and servant, to you two thou- 100
sand.

SPEED, ⌐*aside*⌐   He should give her interest, and she
gives it him.

VALENTINE
As you enjoined me, I have writ your letter
Unto the secret, nameless friend of yours,   105
Which I was much unwilling to proceed in
But for my duty to your Ladyship.
                                    ⌐*He gives her a paper.*⌐

SYLVIA
I thank you, gentle servant, 'tis very clerkly done.

VALENTINE
Now trust me, madam, it came hardly off,
For, being ignorant to whom it goes,   110
I writ at random, very doubtfully.

SYLVIA
Perchance you think too much of so much pains?

VALENTINE
No, madam. So it stead you, I will write,
Please you command, a thousand times as much,
And yet—   115

SYLVIA
A pretty period. Well, I guess the sequel;
And yet I will not name it. And yet I care not.

123. **quaintly:** elegantly; skillfully
128. **I will none of them:** i.e., I don't want them
134. **for your labor:** i.e., as payment
139. **sues:** pleads, appeals

A Milanese lady.
From Cesare Vecellio, *Degli habiti antichi et moderni* . . . (1590).

And yet take this again. ⌜*She holds out the paper.*⌝
  And yet I thank you,
Meaning henceforth to trouble you no more.   120
SPEED, ⌜*aside*⌝
And yet you will; and yet another "yet."
VALENTINE
What means your Ladyship? Do you not like it?
SYLVIA
Yes, yes, the lines are very quaintly writ,
But, since unwillingly, take them again.
Nay, take them.   ⌜*She again offers him the paper.*⌝ 125
VALENTINE   Madam, they are for you.
SYLVIA
Ay, ay. You writ them, sir, at my request,
But I will none of them. They are for you.
I would have had them writ more movingly.
VALENTINE, ⌜*taking the paper*⌝
Please you, I'll write your Ladyship another.   130
SYLVIA
And when it's writ, for my sake read it over,
And if it please you, so; if not, why, so.
VALENTINE If it please me, madam? What then?
SYLVIA
Why, if it please you, take it for your labor.
And so good-morrow, servant.   *Sylvia exits.* 135
SPEED, ⌜*aside*⌝
O jest unseen, inscrutable, invisible
As a nose on a man's face, or a weathercock on a
  steeple!
My master sues to her, and she hath taught her
  suitor,   140
He being her pupil, to become her tutor.
O excellent device! Was there ever heard a better?
That my master, being scribe, to himself should
  write the letter?

145. **reasoning:** talking (Speed's response plays on the proverb "There is neither rhyme nor reason.")

152. **by a figure:** i.e., indirectly (but **a figure** could also mean **a letter** of the alphabet, a meaning that Speed plays on in line 154)

156. **What need she:** i.e., why would she need to

159–60. **perceive her earnest:** i.e., think she was serious (Valentine responds as if **earnest** here were a noun meaning "a pledge in token of a greater gift to come.")

164–65. **there an end:** i.e., there's no more to say

169. **for want of idle time:** i.e., lacking free time; **again reply:** i.e., respond

170. **Or fearing else:** i.e., or else fearing

171. **discover:** reveal, expose

174. **speak in print:** i.e., say precisely, exactly; **in print I found it:** i.e., I read it in a book

176. **have dined:** i.e., have fed on the sight of Sylvia

177. **the chameleon love:** "Love is a chameleon which draweth nothing into the mouth but air" (John Lyly, *Endymion*, 3.4 [1591]). Chameleons were thought to live off air. (See page 58.)

VALENTINE How now, sir? What, are you reasoning 145
with yourself?

SPEED Nay, I was rhyming. 'Tis you that have the
reason.

VALENTINE To do what?

SPEED To be a spokesman from Madam Sylvia. 150

VALENTINE To whom?

SPEED To yourself. Why, she woos you by a figure.

VALENTINE What figure?

SPEED By a letter, I should say.

VALENTINE Why, she hath not writ to me! 155

SPEED What need she when she hath made you write
to yourself? Why, do you not perceive the jest?

VALENTINE No, believe me.

SPEED No believing you indeed, sir. But did you perceive her earnest? 160

VALENTINE She gave me none, except an angry word.

SPEED Why, she hath given you a letter.

VALENTINE That's the letter I writ to her friend.

SPEED And that letter hath she delivered, and there an
end. 165

VALENTINE I would it were no worse.

SPEED I'll warrant you, 'tis as well.
For often have you writ to her, and she, in modesty
Or else for want of idle time, could not again reply,
Or fearing else some messenger that might her 170
mind discover,
Herself hath taught her love himself to write unto
her lover.
All this I speak in print, for in print I found it. Why
muse you, sir? 'Tis dinnertime. 175

VALENTINE I have dined.

SPEED Ay, but hearken, sir, though the chameleon love
can feed on the air, I am one that am nourished by

179. **fain:** gladly; **meat:** food
180. **Be moved:** (1) have compassion; (2) move toward the dinner table

2.2 Proteus takes his leave of Julia, promising to be faithful and sealing their love with a kind of "hand-fasting" or betrothal.

---

4. **turn not:** do not change or alter; do not become fickle or inconstant
7. **seal the bargain:** Proteus and Julia, with their **holy kiss** and the clasping of hands (line 8), perform a version of "handfasting," which constitutes a be-trothal. (Customarily, however, handfasting took place in the presence of witnesses.)
9. **o'erslips me:** slips by me
13. **stays:** awaits
14. **The tide:** i.e., the high **tide** needed for the ship to sail
15. **stay:** delay, detain
19. **grace:** adorn, embellish
20. **you are stayed for:** i.e., they are waiting for you

my victuals and would fain have meat. O, be not like
your mistress! Be moved, be moved.　　　　　　　180

They exit.

Scene 2
Enter Proteus ⌈and⌉ Julia.

PROTEUS　Have patience, gentle Julia.

JULIA　I must where is no remedy.

PROTEUS
When possibly I can, I will return.

JULIA
If you turn not, you will return the sooner.
Keep this remembrance for thy Julia's sake.　　　　5

⌈*She gives him a ring.*⌉

PROTEUS, ⌈*giving her a ring*⌉
Why, then we'll make exchange. Here, take you this.

JULIA
And seal the bargain with a holy kiss.

PROTEUS
Here is my hand for my true constancy.
And when that hour o'erslips me in the day
Wherein I sigh not, Julia, for thy sake,　　　　　　10
The next ensuing hour some foul mischance
Torment me for my love's forgetfulness.
My father stays my coming. Answer not.
The tide is now—nay, not thy tide of tears;
That tide will stay me longer than I should.　　　　15
Julia, farewell.　　　　　　　　　　　　⌈*Julia exits.*⌉
　　　　　　What, gone without a word?
Ay, so true love should do. It cannot speak,
For truth hath better deeds than words to grace it.

⌈*Enter*⌉ *Pantino.*

PANTINO　Sir Proteus, you are stayed for.　　　　20

2.3   Lance grieves that he must part from his family to travel with Proteus, and he chastises his dog, Crab, for not sharing his grief.

———————

2. **kind:** family

3. **received . . . Son:** an allusion to the parable of the Prodigal Son (Luke 15.11–32), which begins with the son saying, "Father, give me the portion of the goods that falleth to me. So he divided unto them his substance." (See page 56.) **proportion:** his error for "portion"

4. **Imperial's:** his error for "Emperor's"

5. **sourest-natured:** The word **crab,** through its link to the sour crab apple, meant "sour-natured."

8. **house:** household, family

10. **a stone:** Proverbial: "A heart as hard as a **stone.**" **pibble:** pebble

11. **A Jew . . . wept:** Proverbial: "It would make a Jew rue." (That there was such a proverb indicates how widespread anti-Semitism was in Shakespeare's time.)

13. **look you:** a phrase used to request attention (but here set in the context of the **grandam** who is **blind**)

18. **worser sole:** probably wordplay on the supposed inferiority of the female soul; **hole:** probably an obscene joke about female anatomy

21. **small:** slender

PROTEUS Go. I come, I come.
⌈*Aside.*⌉ Alas, this parting strikes poor lovers dumb.
                                                        They exit.

Scene 3
Enter Lance, ⌈weeping, with his dog, Crab.⌉

LANCE Nay, 'twill be this hour ere I have done weeping.
All the kind of the Lances have this very fault. I have
received my proportion like the Prodigious Son and
am going with Sir Proteus to the Imperial's court. I
think Crab my dog be the sourest-natured dog that   5
lives: my mother weeping, my father wailing, my
sister crying, our maid howling, our cat wringing
her hands, and all our house in a great perplexity,
yet did not this cruel-hearted cur shed one tear. He
is a stone, a very pibble stone, and has no more pity   10
in him than a dog. A Jew would have wept to have
seen our parting. Why, my grandam, having no
eyes, look you, wept herself blind at my parting.
Nay, I'll show you the manner of it. ⌈*He takes off his
shoes.*⌉ This shoe is my father. No, this left shoe is   15
my father; no, no, this left shoe is my mother. Nay,
that cannot be so neither. Yes, it is so, it is so; it hath
the worser sole. This shoe with the hole in it is my
mother; and this my father. A vengeance on 't, there
'tis! Now sir, this staff is my sister, for, look you, she   20
is as white as a lily and as small as a wand. This hat
is Nan, our maid. I am the dog. No, the dog is
himself, and I am the dog. O, the dog is me, and I
am myself. Ay, so, so. Now come I to my father:
"Father, your blessing." Now should not the shoe   25
speak a word for weeping. Now should I kiss my
father. ⌈*He kisses one shoe.*⌉ Well, he weeps on. Now

29. **wold:** a form of the word "old," already obsolete in Shakespeare's time (See longer note, page 190.)

31. **up and down:** in every respect; precisely

36. **shipped:** embarked, aboard the ship; **post after with oars:** i.e., hurry after him in the rowboat used to get to a ship at anchor

39. **if the tied were lost:** The quibble on **tide** and **tied** continues through line 42.

43. **lose the flood:** i.e., miss high tide

46. **service:** situation or place as a servant

The story of the Prodigal Son. (2.3.3)
From [Guillaume Guéroult,] *Figures de la Bible* . . . (1565–70).

come I to my mother. O, that she could speak now
like a ⌐wold⌐ woman! Well, I kiss her. ⌐*He kisses the
other shoe.*⌐ Why, there 'tis; here's my mother's   30
breath up and down. Now come I to my sister. Mark
the moan she makes! Now the dog all this while
sheds not a tear nor speaks a word. But see how I
lay the dust with my tears.

⌐*Enter*⌐ *Pantino.*

PANTINO Lance, away, away! Aboard. Thy master is   35
 shipped, and thou art to post after with oars. What's
 the matter? Why weep'st thou, man? Away, ass.
 You'll lose the tide if you tarry any longer.
LANCE It is no matter if the tied were lost, for it is the
 unkindest tied that ever any man tied.   40
PANTINO What's the unkindest tide?
LANCE Why, he that's tied here, Crab my dog.
PANTINO Tut, man. I mean thou'lt lose the flood and, in
 losing the flood, lose thy voyage and, in losing thy
 voyage, lose thy master and, in losing thy master,   45
 lose thy service and, in losing thy service—⌐*Lance
 covers Pantino's mouth.*⌐ Why dost thou stop my
 mouth?
LANCE For fear thou shouldst lose thy tongue.
PANTINO Where should I lose my tongue?   50
LANCE In thy tale.
PANTINO In thy tail!
LANCE Lose the tide, and the voyage, and the master,
 and the service, and the tied. Why, man, if the river
 were dry, I am able to fill it with my tears; if the   55
 wind were down, I could drive the boat with my
 sighs.
PANTINO Come. Come away, man. I was sent to call
 thee.
LANCE Sir, call me what thou dar'st   60

2.4 Proteus arrives and is greeted by Valentine and Sylvia. He immediately falls in love with Sylvia.

———

7. **knocked:** hit, beat

10. **Seem you that:** i.e., do you appear to be that which

16. **instance:** evidence, proof

18. **quote:** observe (pronounced like "coat," allowing the wordplay on **jerkin** and **doublet**)

19. **jerkin:** sleeveless jacket or coat

20. **doublet:** close-fitting jacket (See longer note, page 190, and picture, page 62.)

25. **chameleon:** (1) reptile that can change its skin color; (2) inconstant person (For the belief that the **chameleon** lived off **air** [line 27], see note to 2.1.177.) See picture below.

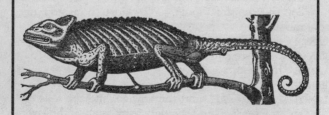

A chameleon. (2.1.177, 2.4.25)
From Edward Topsell, *The history of four-footed beasts and serpents . . .* (1658).

PANTINO   Wilt thou go?
LANCE   Well, I will go.

They exit.

Scene 4
Enter Valentine, Sylvia, Thurio, ⌈and⌉ Speed.

SYLVIA   Servant!
VALENTINE   Mistress?
SPEED   Master, Sir Thurio frowns on you.
VALENTINE   Ay, boy, it's for love.
SPEED   Not of you.   5
VALENTINE   Of my mistress, then.
SPEED   'Twere good you knocked him.
SYLVIA, ⌈*to Valentine*⌉   Servant, you are sad.
VALENTINE   Indeed, madam, I seem so.
THURIO   Seem you that you are not?   10
VALENTINE   Haply I do.
THURIO   So do counterfeits.
VALENTINE   So do you.
THURIO   What seem I that I am not?
VALENTINE   Wise.   15
THURIO   What instance of the contrary?
VALENTINE   Your folly.
THURIO   And how quote you my folly?
VALENTINE   I quote it in your jerkin.
THURIO   My "jerkin" is a doublet.   20
VALENTINE   Well, then, I'll double your folly.
THURIO   How!
SYLVIA   What, angry, Sir Thurio? Do you change color?
VALENTINE   Give him leave, madam. He is a kind of
    chameleon.   25
THURIO   That hath more mind to feed on your blood
    than live in your air.

28. **You have said:** i.e., you've finished your speech

29. **and done too:** Proverbial: "No sooner **said** than **done**" and "So **said** so **done**."

32. **volley:** literally, a discharge of firearms

36. **gave the fire:** applied the flame (to the gunpowder)

38. **kindly:** properly, fittingly

42. **exchequer:** literally, a royal or national treasury

44. **bare liveries:** threadbare uniforms

45. **bare words:** i.e., **words** alone

48. **hard beset:** strenuously assailed (referring to her two suitors)

53. **any happy messenger:** i.e., anything bringing good news

56. **worthy estimation:** i.e., of excellent reputation

57. **not without desert:** i.e., deservedly

VALENTINE   You have said, sir.

THURIO   Ay, sir, and done too for this time.

VALENTINE   I know it well, sir. You always end ere you   30
begin.

SYLVIA   A fine volley of words, gentlemen, and quickly
shot off.

VALENTINE   'Tis indeed, madam. We thank the giver.

SYLVIA   Who is that, servant?   35

VALENTINE   Yourself, sweet lady, for you gave the fire.
Sir Thurio borrows his wit from your Ladyship's
looks and spends what he borrows kindly in your
company.

THURIO   Sir, if you spend word for word with me, I shall   40
make your wit bankrupt.

VALENTINE   I know it well, sir. You have an exchequer
of words and, I think, no other treasure to give your
followers, for it appears by their bare liveries that
they live by your bare words.   45

SYLVIA
No more, gentlemen, no more. Here comes my
father.

⌈*Enter*⌉ *Duke.*

DUKE
Now, daughter Sylvia, you are hard beset.—
Sir Valentine, your father is in good health.
What say you to a letter from your friends   50
Of much good news?

VALENTINE   My lord, I will be thankful
To any happy messenger from thence.

DUKE
Know you Don Antonio, your countryman?

VALENTINE
Ay, my good lord, I know the gentleman   55
To be of worth and worthy estimation,
And not without desert so well reputed.

65. **Omitting:** neglecting

69. **but young:** i.e., no more than **young**

70. **unmellowed:** i.e., not yet mature (perhaps, not yet gray)

72. **Comes:** i.e., come

73. **feature:** i.e., body (literally, shape, proportions)

75. **Beshrew me:** a mild oath; **make this good:** fulfill your promises

77. **meet:** suitable

85. **cite:** i.e., urge

86. **send him:** i.e., **send** Proteus

Man wearing doublet and hose. (2.4.20)
From George Silver, *Paradoxes of defence* (1599).

DUKE   Hath he not a son?

VALENTINE
  Ay, my good lord, a son that well deserves
  The honor and regard of such a father.   60

DUKE   You know him well?

VALENTINE
  I knew him as myself, for from our infancy
  We have conversed and spent our hours together,
  And though myself have been an idle truant,
  Omitting the sweet benefit of time   65
  To clothe mine age with angel-like perfection,
  Yet hath Sir Proteus—for that's his name—
  Made use and fair advantage of his days:
  His years but young, but his experience old;
  His head unmellowed, but his judgment ripe;   70
  And in a word—for far behind his worth
  Comes all the praises that I now bestow—
  He is complete in feature and in mind,
  With all good grace to grace a gentleman.

DUKE
  Beshrew me, sir, but if he make this good,   75
  He is as worthy for an empress' love,
  As meet to be an emperor's counselor.
  Well, sir, this gentleman is come to me
  With commendation from great potentates,
  And here he means to spend his time awhile.   80
  I think 'tis no unwelcome news to you.

VALENTINE
  Should I have wished a thing, it had been he.

DUKE
  Welcome him then according to his worth.
  Sylvia, I speak to you—and you, Sir Thurio.
  For Valentine, I need not cite him to it.   85
  I will send him hither to you presently. ⌜*Duke exits.*⌝

VALENTINE
  This is the gentleman I told your Ladyship

88. Had come: i.e., would have come

90. Belike that: i.e., perhaps

91. Upon . . . fealty: i.e., on receiving another pledge of loyalty

95. love: i.e., a lover (For the wordplay on **love** and **Love** [line 96], see note to 1.1.40.)

98. wink: close his eyes

104. entertain him: i.e., take him into your service

108. have a look of: i.e., receive a glance from

A Milanese young gentleman.
From Cesare Negri, *Nuoue inuentioni di balli* . . . (1604).

Had come along with me but that his mistress
Did hold his eyes locked in her crystal looks.

SYLVIA
Belike that now she hath enfranchised them   90
Upon some other pawn for fealty.

VALENTINE
Nay, sure, I think she holds them prisoners still.

SYLVIA
Nay, then, he should be blind, and being blind
How could he see his way to seek out you?

VALENTINE
Why, lady, love hath twenty pair of eyes.   95

THURIO
They say that Love hath not an eye at all.

VALENTINE
To see such lovers, Thurio, as yourself.
Upon a homely object, Love can wink.

SYLVIA
Have done, have done. Here comes the gentleman.

⌜Enter⌝ Proteus.

VALENTINE
Welcome, dear Proteus.—Mistress, I beseech you   100
Confirm his welcome with some special favor.

SYLVIA
His worth is warrant for his welcome hither,
If this be he you oft have wished to hear from.

VALENTINE
Mistress, it is. Sweet lady, entertain him
To be my fellow-servant to your Ladyship.   105

SYLVIA
Too low a mistress for so high a servant.

PROTEUS
Not so, sweet lady, but too mean a servant
To have a look of such a worthy mistress.

109. **discourse of disability:** i.e., discussion of your unworthiness

112. **want his meed:** i.e., lack its reward

114. **die on him:** i.e., fight anyone to the death

125–26. **have them much commended:** i.e., have sent their warmest greetings

Cupid, the Roman god of love. (1.1.40)
From Henry Peacham, *Minerua Britanna* . . . [1612].

VALENTINE
  Leave off discourse of disability.
  Sweet lady, entertain him for your servant.   110
PROTEUS
  My duty will I boast of, nothing else.
SYLVIA
  And duty never yet did want his meed.
  Servant, you are welcome to a worthless mistress.
PROTEUS
  I'll die on him that says so but yourself.
SYLVIA   That you are welcome?   115
PROTEUS   That you are worthless.

⌈*Enter Servant.*⌉

⌈SERVANT⌉
  Madam, my lord your father would speak with you.
SYLVIA
  I wait upon his pleasure. ⌈*Servant exits.*⌉ Come, Sir
    Thurio,
  Go with me.—Once more, new servant, welcome.   120
  I'll leave you to confer of home affairs.
  When you have done, we look to hear from you.
PROTEUS
  We'll both attend upon your Ladyship.
                            ⌈*Sylvia and Thurio exit.*⌉
VALENTINE
  Now tell me, how do all from whence you came?
PROTEUS
  Your friends are well and have them much   125
    commended.
VALENTINE
  And how do yours?
PROTEUS   I left them all in health.
VALENTINE
  How does your lady? And how thrives your love?

133. **contemning:** disdaining, scorning

139. **watchers:** (1) observers; (2) sleepless companions

142. **as:** i.e., that

143. **to his correction:** i.e., in comparison with his punishment

144. **to his service:** i.e., in comparison with serving him

147. **very naked:** i.e., mere

152. **divine:** That Valentine means "of the nature of a god, godlike" (instead of "excellent," "of surpassing beauty," or any of the other secular meanings of the word) becomes clear at lines 157–59.

153. **flatter her:** praise her unduly or insincerely

154. **flatter me:** say things that please me

PROTEUS
  My tales of love were wont to weary you.   130
  I know you joy not in a love discourse.
VALENTINE
  Ay, Proteus, but that life is altered now.
  I have done penance for contemning Love,
  Whose high imperious thoughts have punished me
  With bitter fasts, with penitential groans,   135
  With nightly tears, and daily heartsore sighs,
  For in revenge of my contempt of love,
  Love hath chased sleep from my enthrallèd eyes
  And made them watchers of mine own heart's
    sorrow.   140
  O gentle Proteus, Love's a mighty lord
  And hath so humbled me as I confess
  There is no woe to his correction,
  Nor, to his service, no such joy on earth.
  Now, no discourse except it be of love.   145
  Now can I break my fast, dine, sup, and sleep
  Upon the very naked name of Love.
PROTEUS
  Enough; I read your fortune in your eye.
  Was this the idol that you worship so?
VALENTINE
  Even she. And is she not a heavenly saint?   150
PROTEUS
  No, but she is an earthly paragon.
VALENTINE
  Call her divine.
PROTEUS   I will not flatter her.
VALENTINE
  O, flatter me, for love delights in praises.
PROTEUS
  When I was sick, you gave me bitter pills,   155
  And I must minister the like to you.

157. **by her:** i.e., of her

158. **principality:** i.e., one of the orders of the angels (Angels are not technically considered **divine.**)

162. **Except . . . against:** unless you wish to take exception to

163. **prefer mine own:** favor my own, like my own better (But **prefer** is used by Valentine in line 164 to mean "advance, promote.")

169. **root:** i.e., furnish with roots

171. **braggartism:** bragging

172. **can:** i.e., can say

173. **To:** i.e., in comparison to

175. **alone:** unique (but Proteus uses it in line 176 in a phrase that means "leave her to herself")

181. **do not dream on thee:** perhaps, ignore you

184. **for:** because

VALENTINE
  Then speak the truth by her; if not divine,
  Yet let her be a principality,
  Sovereign to all the creatures on the earth.
PROTEUS
  Except my mistress.   160
VALENTINE   Sweet, except not any,
  Except thou wilt except against my love.
PROTEUS
  Have I not reason to prefer mine own?
VALENTINE
  And I will help thee to prefer her too:
  She shall be dignified with this high honor—   165
  To bear my lady's train, lest the base earth
  Should from her vesture chance to steal a kiss
  And, of so great a favor growing proud,
  Disdain to root the summer-swelling flower
  And make rough winter everlastingly.   170
PROTEUS
  Why, Valentine, what braggartism is this?
VALENTINE
  Pardon me, Proteus, all I can is nothing
  To her whose worth ⌈makes⌉ other worthies
    nothing.
  She is alone—   175
PROTEUS   Then let her alone.
VALENTINE
  Not for the world! Why, man, she is mine own,
  And I as rich in having such a jewel
  As twenty seas if all their sand were pearl,
  The water nectar, and the rocks pure gold.   180
  Forgive me that I do not dream on thee,
  Because thou seest me dote upon my love.
  My foolish rival, that her father likes
  Only for his possessions are so huge.

185. **after:** i.e., go **after** them
191. **Determined of:** decided, resolved upon
196. **inquire you forth:** seek you out
197. **road:** harbor
202–5. **Even . . . forgotten:** These lines combine three proverbial expressions: "One fire drives out another," "one nail drives out another," and "one love drives out another."
208. **reasonless:** irrationally; without cause
209. **fair:** beautiful
211. **'gainst:** exposed to
213. **Methinks:** it seems to me
217, 218. **advice:** deliberation

Is gone with her along, and I must after,   185
For love, thou know'st, is full of jealousy.
PROTEUS   But she loves you?
VALENTINE
   Ay, and we are betrothed; nay more, our marriage
   hour,
   With all the cunning manner of our flight   190
   Determined of: how I must climb her window,
   The ladder made of cords, and all the means
   Plotted and 'greed on for my happiness.
   Good Proteus, go with me to my chamber,
   In these affairs to aid me with thy counsel.   195
PROTEUS
   Go on before. I shall inquire you forth.
   I must unto the road to disembark
   Some necessaries that I needs must use,
   And then I'll presently attend you.
VALENTINE   Will you make haste?   200
PROTEUS   I will.   ⌈*Valentine and Speed*⌉ *exit.*
   Even as one heat another heat expels,
   Or as one nail by strength drives out another,
   So the remembrance of my former love
   Is by a newer object quite forgotten.   205
   ⌈Is it⌉ mine ⌈eye,⌉ or Valentine's praise,
   Her true perfection, or my false transgression,
   That makes me reasonless to reason thus?
   She is fair, and so is Julia that I love—
   That I did love, for now my love is thawed,   210
   Which like a waxen image 'gainst a fire
   Bears no impression of the thing it was.
   Methinks my zeal to Valentine is cold,
   And that I love him not as I was wont.
   O, but I love his lady too too much,   215
   And that's the reason I love him so little.
   How shall I dote on her with more advice
   That thus without advice begin to love her?

219. **picture:** Editors disagree about whether this is a slip on Shakespeare's part, or whether the word means, unusually, "mere outer appearance," in contrast to **her perfections** or inner beauty (line 221).

220. **dazzled:** confused, dimmed

222. **no reason but:** no possibility but that

224. **compass:** win, obtain

2.5 Lance describes for Speed the tender parting of Proteus from Julia and hears about Valentine's love for Sylvia.

———————

1. **Padua:** In a play filled with inconsistencies, this misplacing of the action from Milan to **Padua** is perhaps the most egregious.

2. **Forswear not thyself:** i.e., don't perjure yourself (by swearing that Lance is **welcome**)

4. **undone:** ruined; **never:** i.e., ever

5. **shot:** reckoning, bill

11. **closed in earnest:** embraced sincerely

12. **fairly:** peaceably; **in jest:** as opposed to **"in earnest"**

17. **are they broken:** i.e., have they quarreled

18. **whole as a fish:** This proverb means "in good health," but Lance plays on the meaning of **whole** as "not **broken**."

20. **stands well with him:** probably a bawdy reference

23. **block:** blockhead

'Tis but her picture I have yet beheld,
And that hath dazzled my reason's light;   220
But when I look on her perfections,
There is no reason but I shall be blind.
If I can check my erring love, I will;
If not, to compass her I'll use my skill.

⌜*He*⌝ *exits.*

Scene 5
Enter Speed and Lance, ⌜*with his dog, Crab.*⌝

SPEED   Lance, by mine honesty, welcome to Padua.

LANCE   Forswear not thyself, sweet youth, for I am not
welcome. I reckon this always: that a man is never
undone till he be hanged, nor never welcome to a
place till some certain shot be paid and the Hostess   5
say welcome.

SPEED   Come on, you madcap. I'll to the alehouse with
you presently, where, for one shot of five pence,
thou shalt have five thousand welcomes. But, sirrah,
how did thy master part with Madam Julia?   10

LANCE   Marry, after they closed in earnest, they parted
very fairly in jest.

SPEED   But shall she marry him?

LANCE   No.

SPEED   How then? Shall he marry her?   15

LANCE   No, neither.

SPEED   What, are they broken?

LANCE   No, they are both as whole as a fish.

SPEED   Why then, how stands the matter with them?

LANCE   Marry, thus: when it stands well with him, it   20
stands well with her.

SPEED   What an ass art thou! I understand thee not.

LANCE   What a block art thou that thou canst not! My
staff understands me.

26. **but:** merely

37. **parable:** enigmatic saying

38–39. **how sayst thou:** i.e., what do you think of the fact

43. **mistak'st me:** misunderstand my words (Lance responds as if the words had meant "have the wrong view of my character.")

52. **ale:** (1) "church-ale," a festival to raise money for a church; or (2) **alehouse** (See page 134.)

2.6 Proteus decides to betray Valentine's elopement plans to Sylvia's father as a step on the way to winning Sylvia for himself.

———

1. **shall I be forsworn:** i.e., I shall have perjured myself

"My master is become a hot lover." (2.5.45)
From Gilles Corrozet, *Hecatongraphie* . . . (1543).

SPEED   What thou sayst?   25
LANCE   Ay, and what I do too. Look thee, I'll but lean,
and my staff understands me.
SPEED   It stands under thee indeed.
LANCE   Why, "stand under" and "understand" is all
one.   30
SPEED   But tell me true, will 't be a match?
LANCE   Ask my dog. If he say "Ay," it will; if he say
"No," it will; if he shake his tail and say nothing, it
will.
SPEED   The conclusion is, then, that it will.   35
LANCE   Thou shalt never get such a secret from me but
by a parable.
SPEED   'Tis well that I get it so. But, Lance, how sayst
thou that my master is become a notable lover?
LANCE   I never knew him otherwise.   40
SPEED   Than how?
LANCE   A notable lubber, as thou reportest him to be.
SPEED   Why, thou whoreson ass, thou mistak'st me.
LANCE   Why, fool, I meant not thee; I meant thy master.
SPEED   I tell thee, my master is become a hot lover.   45
LANCE   Why, I tell thee, I care not though he burn
himself in love. If thou wilt, go with me to the
alehouse; if not, thou art an Hebrew, a Jew, and not
worth the name of a Christian.
SPEED   Why?   50
LANCE   Because thou hast not so much charity in thee
as to go to the ale with a Christian. Wilt thou go?
SPEED   At thy service.
                                                They exit.

                            Scene 6
                    Enter Proteus alone.

PROTEUS
To leave my Julia, shall I be forsworn.
To love fair Sylvia, shall I be forsworn.

5. **Provokes:** incites, urges

7. **sweet-suggesting:** i.e., sweetly suggestive; **if thou hast:** i.e., if you have ever

8. **excuse it:** i.e., justify my behavior, vindicate myself (His justifications begin at line 9.)

11. **Unheedful:** heedless

12. **wants:** lacks

13. **learn:** teach

14. **unreverend:** irreverent

15. **preferred:** held out, recommended

16. **soul-confirming:** i.e., soul-confirmed

17. **leave:** cease

24. **still:** always

26. **Shows Julia:** makes **Julia** look like (in comparison); **Ethiope:** In sixteenth-century England, where fair skin was equated with beauty, the dark-skinned African was often singled out as beauty's opposite.

32. **used to:** i.e., employed against

34. **climb:** i.e., climb up to

35. **in counsel:** in secret, in private; **competitor:** perhaps, associate, partner; or, perhaps, rival

To wrong my friend, I shall be much forsworn.
And ev'n that power which gave me first my oath
Provokes me to this threefold perjury.   5
Love bade me swear, and love bids me forswear.
O sweet-suggesting Love, if thou hast sinned,
Teach me, thy tempted subject, to excuse it.
At first I did adore a twinkling star,
But now I worship a celestial sun;   10
Unheedful vows may heedfully be broken,
And he wants wit that wants resolvèd will
To learn his wit t' exchange the bad for better.
Fie, fie, unreverend tongue, to call her bad
Whose sovereignty so oft thou hast preferred   15
With twenty thousand soul-confirming oaths.
I cannot leave to love, and yet I do.
But there I leave to love where I should love.
Julia I lose, and Valentine I lose;
If I keep them, I needs must lose myself;   20
If I lose them, thus find I by their loss:
For Valentine, myself; for Julia, Sylvia.
I to myself am dearer than a friend,
For love is still most precious in itself,
And Sylvia—witness heaven that made her fair—   25
Shows Julia but a swarthy Ethiope.
I will forget that Julia is alive,
Rememb'ring that my love to her is dead;
And Valentine I'll hold an enemy,
Aiming at Sylvia as a sweeter friend.   30
I cannot now prove constant to myself
Without some treachery used to Valentine.
This night he meaneth with a corded ladder
To climb celestial Sylvia's chamber window,
Myself in counsel his competitor.   35
Now presently I'll give her father notice

37. **pretended:** purposed, intended
40. **cross:** thwart
41. **blunt:** stupid, obtuse
42. **wings:** Cupid was usually pictured with **wings** to suggest love's swiftness. (See, for example, pages 44 and 136.)
43. **drift:** scheme, design

2.7 Julia decides to follow Proteus to Milan and asks Lucetta to help her disguise herself as a page.

———————

3. **table:** writing tablet
4. **charactered:** accent on second syllable
5. **mean:** i.e., means
6. **with my honor:** i.e., without destroying my reputation
10. **measure:** walk across, traverse

"A true-devoted pilgrim." (2.7.9)
From Henry Peacham, *Minerua Britanna* . . . [1612].

Of their disguising and pretended flight,
Who, all enraged, will banish Valentine,
For Thurio he intends shall wed his daughter.
But Valentine being gone, I'll quickly cross   40
By some sly trick blunt Thurio's dull proceeding.
Love, lend me wings to make my purpose swift,
As thou hast lent me wit to plot this drift.

                                          He exits.

                      Scene 7
               Enter Julia and Lucetta.

JULIA
    Counsel, Lucetta. Gentle girl, assist me;
    And ev'n in kind love I do conjure thee
    Who art the table wherein all my thoughts
    Are visibly charactered and engraved—
    To lesson me and tell me some good mean   5
    How with my honor I may undertake
    A journey to my loving Proteus.
LUCETTA
    Alas, the way is wearisome and long.
JULIA
    A true-devoted pilgrim is not weary
    To measure kingdoms with his feeble steps;   10
    Much less shall she that hath Love's wings to fly,
    And when the flight is made to one so dear,
    Of such divine perfection, as Sir Proteus.
LUCETTA
    Better forbear till Proteus make return.
JULIA
    O, know'st thou not his looks are my soul's food?   15
    Pity the dearth that I have pinèd in
    By longing for that food so long a time.

18. **inly:** inward, heartfelt

22. **qualify:** moderate

24. **thou damm'st it up:** i.e., you confine it (In the lines that follow, the metaphor shifts from the confining of a fire to the damming of a stream.)

27–32. **his, he:** its, it (In these lines, **he** and **his** refer to **the current.**)

29. **sedge:** a grassy plant growing in wet places (See below.)

38. **Elysium:** in Greek mythology, the home of the blessed after death

39. **habit:** clothing

41. **loose:** immoral or licentious

42. **weeds:** apparel

43. **beseem:** befit, be suitable for

45. **knit:** tie

46. **odd-conceited:** strangely devised; **true-love knots:** complicated ornamental **knots**

Sedge. (2.7.29)
From John Gerard, *The herball . . .* (1597).

Didst thou but know the inly touch of love,
Thou wouldst as soon go kindle fire with snow
As seek to quench the fire of love with words.   20

LUCETTA
I do not seek to quench your love's hot fire,
But qualify the fire's extreme rage,
Lest it should burn above the bounds of reason.

JULIA
The more thou damm'st it up, the more it burns.
The current that with gentle murmur glides,   25
Thou know'st, being stopped, impatiently doth rage,
But when his fair course is not hinderèd,
He makes sweet music with th' enameled stones,
Giving a gentle kiss to every sedge
He overtaketh in his pilgrimage;   30
And so by many winding nooks he strays
With willing sport to the wild ocean.
Then let me go and hinder not my course.
I'll be as patient as a gentle stream
And make a pastime of each weary step   35
Till the last step have brought me to my love,
And there I'll rest as after much turmoil
A blessèd soul doth in Elysium.

LUCETTA
But in what habit will you go along?

JULIA
Not like a woman, for I would prevent   40
The loose encounters of lascivious men.
Gentle Lucetta, fit me with such weeds
As may beseem some well-reputed page.

LUCETTA
Why, then, your Ladyship must cut your hair.

JULIA
No, girl, I'll knit it up in silken strings   45
With twenty odd-conceited true-love knots.

47. **fantastic:** fanciful; foppish

48. **greater time:** i.e., more years; **show:** appear; pretend

51. **What compass:** i.e., how large a circumference; **farthingale:** See page 86.

53. **must needs:** i.e., must; **codpiece:** pouch at the crotch of men's breeches, often with **pins** (line 56) and other decorations

54. **Out:** an expression of reproach; **ill-favored:** ugly; offensive

55. **round hose:** close-fitting hose topped with padded breeches around the upper thighs

58. **meet:** proper; **mannerly:** perhaps punning on "manlike"

60. **unstaid:** capricious

64. **dream on:** conceive, imagine, think about

66. **No matter:** i.e., it doesn't **matter**

67. **withal:** i.e., with **your journey**

72. **are servants to:** i.e., can be made use of by

To be fantastic may become a youth
Of greater time than I shall show to be.

LUCETTA
What fashion, madam, shall I make your breeches?

JULIA
That fits as well as "Tell me, good my lord,   50
What compass will you wear your farthingale?"
Why, ev'n what fashion thou best likes, Lucetta.

LUCETTA
You must needs have them with a codpiece, madam.

JULIA
Out, out, Lucetta. That will be ill-favored.

LUCETTA
A round hose, madam, now's not worth a pin   55
Unless you have a codpiece to stick pins on.

JULIA
Lucetta, as thou lov'st me, let me have
What thou think'st meet and is most mannerly.
But tell me, wench, how will the world repute me
For undertaking so unstaid a journey?   60
I fear me it will make me scandalized.

LUCETTA
If you think so, then stay at home and go not.

JULIA   Nay, that I will not.

LUCETTA
Then never dream on infamy, but go.
If Proteus like your journey when you come,   65
No matter who's displeased when you are gone.
I fear me he will scarce be pleased withal.

JULIA
That is the least, Lucetta, of my fear.
A thousand oaths, an ocean of his tears,
And instances of infinite of love   70
Warrant me welcome to my Proteus.

LUCETTA
All these are servants to deceitful men.

86. **at thy dispose:** in your charge or control
88. **in lieu thereof:** i.e., in exchange for which
90. **tarriance:** delay

A woman wearing a farthingale. (2.7.51, 4.4.39)
From John Speed, *The theatre of the empire
of Great Britaine* . . . (1614).

JULIA
Base men that use them to so base effect!
But truer stars did govern Proteus' birth.
His words are bonds, his oaths are oracles,   75
His love sincere, his thoughts immaculate,
His tears pure messengers sent from his heart,
His heart as far from fraud as heaven from earth.

LUCETTA
Pray heav'n he prove so when you come to him.

JULIA
Now, as thou lov'st me, do him not that wrong   80
To bear a hard opinion of his truth.
Only deserve my love by loving him.
And presently go with me to my chamber
To take a note of what I stand in need of
To furnish me upon my longing journey.   85
All that is mine I leave at thy dispose,
My goods, my lands, my reputation.
Only, in lieu thereof, dispatch me hence.
Come, answer not, but to it presently.
I am impatient of my tarriance.   90

They exit.

THE TWO
GENTLEMEN
OF VERONA

ACT 3

3.1 Proteus betrays Valentine's elopement plans to Sylvia's father, who banishes Valentine. Proteus pretends to grieve with Valentine and, telling him that Sylvia has been imprisoned by her father, conveys Valentine on his way into exile.

––––––––––

1. **give us leave:** i.e., leave us
4. **discover:** reveal
8. **pricks me on:** urges me
18. **cross:** thwart; **drift:** scheme
21. **timeless:** untimely, premature

ACT 3

Scene 1
Enter Duke, Thurio, ⌐ *and* ⌐ *Proteus.*

DUKE
Sir Thurio, give us leave, I pray, awhile;
We have some secrets to confer about. ⌐*Thurio exits.*⌐
Now tell me, Proteus, what's your will with me?

PROTEUS
My gracious lord, that which I would discover
The law of friendship bids me to conceal,   5
But when I call to mind your gracious favors
Done to me, undeserving as I am,
My duty pricks me on to utter that
Which else no worldly good should draw from me.
Know, worthy prince, Sir Valentine my friend   10
This night intends to steal away your daughter;
Myself am one made privy to the plot.
I know you have determined to bestow her
On Thurio, whom your gentle daughter hates,
And should she thus be stol'n away from you,   15
It would be much vexation to your age.
Thus, for my duty's sake, I rather chose
To cross my friend in his intended drift
Than, by concealing it, heap on your head
A pack of sorrows which would press you down,   20
Being unprevented, to your timeless grave.

23. **command me:** i.e., call on me for any service

25. **Haply:** perhaps; by chance

28. **jealous aim might err:** i.e., suspicious guess might be wrong

34. **suggested:** seduced, tempted

38. **mean:** means

42. **presently:** now

45. **aimèd at:** i.e., suspected

47. **publisher:** proclaimer, announcer; **pretense:** plan

49. **light:** i.e., news, word

DUKE
Proteus, I thank thee for thine honest care,
Which to requite command me while I live.
This love of theirs myself have often seen,
Haply when they have judged me fast asleep,   25
And oftentimes have purposed to forbid
Sir Valentine her company and my court.
But fearing lest my jealous aim might err
And so, unworthily, disgrace the man—
A rashness that I ever yet have shunned—   30
I gave him gentle looks, thereby to find
That which thyself hast now disclosed to me.
And that thou mayst perceive my fear of this,
Knowing that tender youth is soon suggested,
I nightly lodge her in an upper tower,   35
The key whereof myself have ever kept,
And thence she cannot be conveyed away.

PROTEUS
Know, noble lord, they have devised a mean
How he her chamber-window will ascend
And with a corded ladder fetch her down;   40
For which the youthful lover now is gone,
And this way comes he with it presently,
Where, if it please you, you may intercept him.
But, good my lord, do it so cunningly
That my discovery be not aimèd at;   45
For love of you, not hate unto my friend,
Hath made me publisher of this pretense.

DUKE
Upon mine honor, he shall never know
That I had any light from thee of this.

PROTEUS
Adieu, my lord. Sir Valentine is coming.   50

⌜*Proteus exits.*⌝

52. **Please it your Grace:** a deferential phrase
59. **break with thee of:** i.e., tell you about
60. **touch me near:** concern me closely
63. **sure:** surely
64. **Were:** i.e., would be
65. **virtue:** ability, distinction
66. **Beseeming:** i.e., that are appropriate to
68. **peevish:** headstrong, obstinate
70. **regarding:** taking into account
73. **Upon advice:** after deliberation
74. **where:** i.e., whereas; **mine age:** i.e., the span of my life
76. **full:** i.e., fully
77. **turn her out:** i.e., drive Sylvia out; **who:** i.e., whoever

A jade. (3.1.282)
From Cesare Fiaschi, *Trattato dell'imbrigliare . . .
caualli . . .* (1614).

⌈*Enter*⌉ *Valentine.*

DUKE
Sir Valentine, whither away so fast?
VALENTINE
Please it your Grace, there is a messenger
That stays to bear my letters to my friends,
And I am going to deliver them.
DUKE   Be they of much import?   55
VALENTINE
The tenor of them doth but signify
My health and happy being at your court.
DUKE
Nay then, no matter. Stay with me awhile;
I am to break with thee of some affairs
That touch me near, wherein thou must be secret.   60
'Tis not unknown to thee that I have sought
To match my friend Sir Thurio to my daughter.
VALENTINE
I know it well, my lord, and sure the match
Were rich and honorable. Besides, the gentleman
Is full of virtue, bounty, worth, and qualities   65
Beseeming such a wife as your fair daughter.
Cannot your Grace win her to fancy him?
DUKE
No. Trust me, she is peevish, sullen, froward,
Proud, disobedient, stubborn, lacking duty,
Neither regarding that she is my child   70
Nor fearing me as if I were her father;
And may I say to thee, this pride of hers,
Upon advice, hath drawn my love from her,
And where I thought the remnant of mine age
Should have been cherished by her childlike duty,   75
I now am full resolved to take a wife
And turn her out to who will take her in.
Then let her beauty be her wedding dower,
For me and my possessions she esteems not

81. **Verona:** perhaps an error for Milan (The geography of the action of the play is quite unstable.) See maps of Verona and Milan, pages xv and xvi.

82. **affect:** love; **nice:** shy; or, hard to please

84. **have thee to my tutor:** i.e., like you to instruct me

85. **agone:** ago; **forgot:** i.e., forgotten how

87. **bestow:** conduct

88. **regarded:** held in respect

90. **kind:** nature

91. **quick:** lively

94. **give her o'er:** i.e., give up pursuing her

99. **Forwhy:** because

101. **For:** i.e., by

103. **black:** By Elizabethan standards of beauty, only fair hair and fair skin are beautiful. (See note to 2.6.26.)

104. **That man . . . tongue:** i.e., any man at all

106. **friends:** family

VALENTINE
  What would your Grace have me to do in this?   80
DUKE
  There is a lady in Verona here
  Whom I affect; but she is nice, and coy,
  And nought esteems my agèd eloquence.
  Now therefore would I have thee to my tutor—
  For long agone I have forgot to court;   85
  Besides, the fashion of the time is changed—
  How and which way I may bestow myself
  To be regarded in her sun-bright eye.
VALENTINE
  Win her with gifts if she respect not words;
  Dumb jewels often in their silent kind   90
  More than quick words do move a woman's mind.
DUKE
  But she did scorn a present that I sent her.
VALENTINE
  A woman sometime scorns what best contents her.
  Send her another; never give her o'er,
  For scorn at first makes after-love the more.   95
  If she do frown, 'tis not in hate of you,
  But rather to beget more love in you.
  If she do chide, 'tis not to have you gone,
  Forwhy the fools are mad if left alone.
  Take no repulse, whatever she doth say;   100
  For "get you gone" she doth not mean "away."
  Flatter and praise, commend, extol their graces;
  Though ne'er so black, say they have angels' faces.
  That man that hath a tongue, I say, is no man
  If with his tongue he cannot win a woman.   105
DUKE
  But she I mean is promised by her friends
  Unto a youthful gentleman of worth
  And kept severely from resort of men,
  That no man hath access by day to her.

113. **What lets but one may enter at:** i.e., what would hinder anyone from entering

115. **shelving:** overhanging, projecting

116. **apparent:** obvious, manifest

117. **quaintly:** skillfully

119. **Hero's tower:** In the story of Hero and **Leander,** Hero lives as a priestess of Venus in a **tower** on the banks of the Hellespont. (See note to 1.1.22, and picture, page 18.)

121. **blood:** good parentage; or, perhaps, passion

130. **of any length:** i.e., fairly long (The phrase **of length** meant "long.")

131. **turn:** purpose

Phaëton falling from his "heavenly car." (3.1.157–59)
From Ovid, . . . *Metamorphoseos* . . . (1527).

VALENTINE
Why, then, I would resort to her by night.   110
DUKE
Ay, but the doors be locked and keys kept safe,
That no man hath recourse to her by night.
VALENTINE
What lets but one may enter at her window?
DUKE
Her chamber is aloft, far from the ground,
And built so shelving that one cannot climb it   115
Without apparent hazard of his life.
VALENTINE
Why, then a ladder quaintly made of cords
To cast up, with a pair of anchoring hooks,
Would serve to scale another Hero's tower,
So bold Leander would adventure it.   120
DUKE
Now, as thou art a gentleman of blood,
Advise me where I may have such a ladder.
VALENTINE
When would you use it? Pray sir, tell me that.
DUKE
This very night; for love is like a child
That longs for everything that he can come by.   125
VALENTINE
By seven o'clock I'll get you such a ladder.
DUKE
But hark thee: I will go to her alone;
How shall I best convey the ladder thither?
VALENTINE
It will be light, my lord, that you may bear it
Under a cloak that is of any length.   130
DUKE
A cloak as long as thine will serve the turn?
VALENTINE
Ay, my good lord.

134. **such another:** i.e., the same

140. **an engine fit for my proceeding:** i.e., just the device (the rope ladder) that I need

142. **harbor:** lodge, reside

143. **that:** who

144. **lightly:** easily

145. **senseless:** incapable of sensation

147. **herald thoughts: thoughts** that (1) carry my message, and (2) announce my approach; **them:** themselves

148. **importune:** urge, impel (accent on second syllable)

149. **the grace:** the good fortune; **such grace:** such favor

151. **want:** lack

152. **for:** since

157–59. **Phaëton . . . world: Phaëton** was killed when, trying to drive **the heavenly car** (the chariot of the sun), he lost control and scorched the earth. He was fathered by Apollo, but his mother was married to **Merops.** (See page 98.)

160. **reach:** i.e., reach for

162. **equal mates:** i.e., lovers who would be your social **equal** (but also with the contemptuous sense of **mates** as "fellows")

DUKE   Then let me see thy cloak;
  I'll get me one of such another length.
VALENTINE
  Why, any cloak will serve the turn, my lord.   135
DUKE
  How shall I fashion me to wear a cloak?
  I pray thee, let me feel thy cloak upon me.
                        ⌈*Pulling off the cloak, he reveals
                         a rope ladder and a paper.*⌉
  What letter is this same? What's here? (⌈*Reads.*⌉) *To
    Sylvia.*
  And here an engine fit for my proceeding.   140
  I'll be so bold to break the seal for once.
    (⌈*Reads.*⌉)
  *My thoughts do harbor with my Sylvia nightly,
    And slaves they are to me that send them flying.
  O, could their master come and go as lightly,
    Himself would lodge where, senseless, they are*   145
      *lying.
  My herald thoughts in thy pure bosom rest them,
    While I, their king, that thither them importune,
  Do curse the grace that with such grace hath blest
      them,*   150
    *Because myself do want my servants' fortune.
  I curse myself, for they are sent by me,
  That they should harbor where their lord should be.*
  What's here?
  (⌈*Reads.*⌉) *Sylvia, this night I will enfranchise thee.*   155
  'Tis so. And here's the ladder for the purpose.
  Why, Phaëton—for thou art Merops' son—
  Wilt thou aspire to guide the heavenly car
  And with thy daring folly burn the world?
  Wilt thou reach stars because they shine on thee?   160
  Go, base intruder, overweening slave,
  Bestow thy fawning smiles on equal mates
  And think my patience, more than thy desert,

164. **Is privilege for:** i.e., privileges, authorizes

168. **expedition:** i.e., motion

181. **shadow:** delusive and insubstantial image

182. **Except I be:** i.e., unless I am

186. **leave:** cease

187. **influence:** in astrology, the flowing from the heavens of an ethereal fluid that affects the characters and destinies of humans

189. **his deadly doom:** i.e., the Duke's decree of death

190. **Tarry I:** i.e., if I stay; **but attend on:** i.e., merely serve

193. **So-ho:** a call announcing a discovery (specifically, a hunting call announcing that the hare has been sighted)

A nightingale. (3.1.183, 5.4.5)
From Konrad Gesner, . . . *Historiae animalium* . . . (1585–1604).

Is privilege for thy departure hence.
Thank me for this more than for all the favors   165
Which all too much I have bestowed on thee.
But if thou linger in my territories
Longer than swiftest expedition
Will give thee time to leave our royal court,
By heaven, my wrath shall far exceed the love   170
I ever bore my daughter or thyself.
Begone. I will not hear thy vain excuse,
But, as thou lov'st thy life, make speed from hence.
⌜*He exits.*⌝

VALENTINE
And why not death, rather than living torment?
To die is to be banished from myself,   175
And Sylvia is myself; banished from her
Is self from self—a deadly banishment.
What light is light if Sylvia be not seen?
What joy is joy if Sylvia be not by—
Unless it be to think that she is by   180
And feed upon the shadow of perfection?
Except I be by Sylvia in the night,
There is no music in the nightingale.
Unless I look on Sylvia in the day,
There is no day for me to look upon.   185
She is my essence, and I leave to be
If I be not by her fair influence
Fostered, illumined, cherished, kept alive.
I fly not death, to fly his deadly doom;
Tarry I here, I but attend on death,   190
But fly I hence, I fly away from life.

⌜*Enter*⌝ *Proteus* ⌜*and*⌝ *Lance.*

PROTEUS   Run, boy, run, run, and seek him out.
LANCE   So-ho, so-ho!
PROTEUS   What seest thou?

195. **Him:** i.e., he whom

195–96. **There's . . . 'tis:** i.e., every hair on his head is (with a pun on **hair**/hare)

206. **Villain:** literally, peasant, but referring to any social inferior; **forbear:** i.e., stop (Lance apparently makes some move toward striking Valentine.)

212. **they:** i.e., the **news; untunable:** harsh-sounding

An image of despair. (3.1.253)
From Jean Francois Senault, *The use of passions* . . . (1649).

LANCE Him we go to find. There's not a hair on 's head 195
    but 'tis a Valentine.

PROTEUS Valentine?

VALENTINE No.

PROTEUS Who then? His spirit?

VALENTINE Neither. 200

PROTEUS What then?

VALENTINE Nothing.

LANCE Can nothing speak? Master, shall I strike?

PROTEUS Who wouldst thou strike?

LANCE Nothing. 205

PROTEUS Villain, forbear.

LANCE Why, sir, I'll strike nothing. I pray you—

PROTEUS
    Sirrah, I say forbear.—Friend Valentine, a word.

VALENTINE
    My ears are stopped and cannot hear good news,
    So much of bad already hath possessed them. 210

PROTEUS
    Then in dumb silence will I bury mine,
    For they are harsh, untunable, and bad.

VALENTINE Is Sylvia dead?

PROTEUS No, Valentine.

VALENTINE
    No Valentine indeed for sacred Sylvia. 215
    Hath she forsworn me?

PROTEUS No, Valentine.

VALENTINE
    No Valentine if Sylvia have forsworn me.
    What is your news?

LANCE Sir, there is a proclamation that you are van- 220
    ished.

PROTEUS
    That thou art banishèd—O, that's the news—
    From hence, from Sylvia, and from me thy friend.

225. **surfeit:** overindulge

227. **doom:** decree

228. **unreversed:** i.e., if not reversed

230. **tendered:** i.e., offered (along with **her humble self** [line 231]) as payment or ransom

240. **repeal:** recall from banishment

241. **close prison:** i.e., strict confinement in prison

242. **biding:** remaining

246. **ending anthem:** In "The Phoenix and the Turtle," a poem probably by Shakespeare, the word **anthem** means "requiem," or hymn for the dead, and probably means that here as well.

247. **that:** that which

248. **study:** i.e., think about

253. **manage:** wield

VALENTINE

O, I have fed upon this woe already,
And now excess of it will make me surfeit.   22⁵
Doth Sylvia know that I am banishèd?

PROTEUS

Ay, ay, and she hath offered to the doom—
Which unreversed stands in effectual force—
A sea of melting pearl, which some call tears;
Those at her father's churlish feet she tendered,   23⁰
With them, upon her knees, her humble self,
Wringing her hands, whose whiteness so became
   them
As if but now they waxèd pale for woe.
But neither bended knees, pure hands held up,   23⁵
Sad sighs, deep groans, nor silver-shedding tears
Could penetrate her uncompassionate sire;
But Valentine, if he be ta'en, must die.
Besides, her intercession chafed him so,
When she for thy repeal was suppliant,   240
That to close prison he commanded her
With many bitter threats of biding there.

VALENTINE

No more, unless the next word that thou speak'st
Have some malignant power upon my life.
If so, I pray thee breathe it in mine ear   245
As ending anthem of my endless dolor.

PROTEUS

Cease to lament for that thou canst not help,
And study help for that which thou lament'st.
Time is the nurse and breeder of all good.
Here, if thou stay, thou canst not see thy love;   250
Besides, thy staying will abridge thy life.
Hope is a lover's staff; walk hence with that
And manage it against despairing thoughts.
Thy letters may be here, though thou art hence,
Which, being writ to me, shall be delivered   255

257. **expostulate:** talk at length

259. **confer at large:** talk with you fully

261. **though not for thyself:** i.e., even if not for your own sake

262. **along:** i.e., come

263. **my boy:** i.e., Speed

269–70. **that's all one:** i.e., that doesn't matter

270. **but:** only; **He lives not now:** i.e., there's no one alive

275. **maid:** Lance plays on **maid** as (1) virgin; (2) maidservant; **gossips:** sponsors at her child's baptism

277. **qualities:** accomplishments

278. **bare:** (1) mere; (2) hairless

279. **catalog:** list

280. **Imprimis:** Latin for "in the first place," used to introduce a list of items

282. **jade:** (1) broken-down horse (See page 94.) (2) hussy

283. **Item:** i.e., also (used to introduce each thing enumerated in a list)

Even in the milk-white bosom of thy love.
The time now serves not to expostulate.
Come, I'll convey thee through the city gate
And, ere I part with thee, confer at large
Of all that may concern thy love affairs.   260
As thou lov'st Sylvia, though not for thyself,
Regard thy danger, and along with me.

VALENTINE
I pray thee, Lance, an if thou seest my boy,
Bid him make haste and meet me at the North
    Gate.   265

PROTEUS
Go, sirrah, find him out.—Come, Valentine.

VALENTINE
O, my dear Sylvia! Hapless Valentine!
                        ⌜*Valentine and Proteus exit.*⌝

LANCE   I am but a fool, look you, and yet I have the wit
to think my master is a kind of a knave, but that's all
one if he be but one knave. He lives not now that   270
knows me to be in love, yet I am in love, but a team
of horse shall not pluck that from me, nor who 'tis I
love; and yet 'tis a woman, but what woman I will
not tell myself; and yet 'tis a milk-maid; yet 'tis not a
maid, for she hath had gossips; yet 'tis a maid, for   275
she is her master's maid and serves for wages. She
hath more qualities than a water spaniel, which is
much in a bare Christian. ⌜*He takes out a piece of
paper.*⌝ Here is the catalog of her condition.
(⌜*Reads.*⌝) *Imprimis, She can fetch and carry.* Why, a   280
horse can do no more; nay, a horse cannot fetch but
only carry; therefore is she better than a jade.
(⌜*Reads.*⌝) *Item, She can milk.* Look you, a sweet
virtue in a maid with clean hands.

                        ⌜*Enter*⌝ Speed.

SPEED   How now, Signior Lance? What news with your   285
Mastership?

293. **them:** i.e., the **news** (line 289)

294. **jolt-head:** blockhead

296, 300. **try:** test, put to the proof

301–2. **Saint Nicholas:** the patron of scholars, especially schoolboys

302. **thy speed:** the promoter of your success, with a pun on Speed's name

311. **stock:** dowry

312. **stock:** stocking

315. **scoured:** (1) scrubbed; (2) beaten

317. **set the world on wheels:** i.e., take it easy (See below.)

To "set the world on wheels." (3.1.317)
From John Taylor, *All the Workes of . . .* (1630).

LANCE   With my master's ship? Why, it is at sea.

SPEED   Well, your old vice still: mistake the word. What news, then, in your paper?

LANCE   The black'st news that ever thou heard'st.   290

SPEED   Why, man? How black?

LANCE   Why, as black as ink.

SPEED   Let me read them.

LANCE   Fie on thee, jolt-head, thou canst not read.

SPEED   Thou liest. I can.   295

LANCE   I will try thee. Tell me this, who begot thee?

SPEED   Marry, the son of my grandfather.

LANCE   O, illiterate loiterer, it was the son of thy grand-mother. This proves that thou canst not read.

SPEED   Come, fool, come. Try me in thy paper.   300

LANCE, ⌈*giving him the paper*⌉ There, and Saint Nicholas be thy speed.

SPEED ⌈*reads*⌉ *Imprimis, She can milk.*

LANCE   Ay, that she can.

SPEED   *Item, She brews good ale.*   305

LANCE   And thereof comes the proverb: "Blessing of your heart, you brew good ale."

SPEED   *Item, She can sew.*

LANCE   That's as much as to say "Can she so?"

SPEED   *Item, She can knit.*   310

LANCE   What need a man care for a stock with a wench, when she can knit him a stock?

SPEED   *Item, She can wash and scour.*

LANCE   A special virtue, for then she need not be washed and scoured.   315

SPEED   *Item, She can spin.*

LANCE   Then may I set the world on wheels, when she can spin for her living.

SPEED   *Item, She hath many nameless virtues.*

LANCE   That's as much as to say "bastard virtues," that   320 indeed know not their fathers and therefore have no names.

325. **in respect of:** as relates to or regards

329. **hath a sweet mouth:** i.e., likes sweets (also, perhaps, is lecherous)

336. **only:** preeminent

339. **Eve's legacy:** i.e., her inheritance from Eve, her nature as a woman

343. **curst:** shrewish (Lance responds to a second meaning, "savage.")

345. **praise:** appraise, test (by drinking)

347. **praised:** extolled, spoken highly of

348. **liberal:** licentious (Lance responds to a second meaning, "generous.")

356. **Rehearse:** repeat

"She can milk." (3.1.283, 303)
From Pietro de Crescenzi, [Ruralia commoda, 1561].

SPEED   Here follow her vices.

LANCE   Close at the heels of her virtues.

SPEED   *Item, She is not to be ⌈kissed⌉ fasting in respect of* 325
her breath.

LANCE   Well, that fault may be mended with a breakfast.
Read on.

SPEED   *Item, She hath a sweet mouth.*

LANCE   That makes amends for her sour breath.   330

SPEED   *Item, She doth talk in her sleep.*

LANCE   It's no matter for that, so she sleep not in her
talk.

SPEED   *Item, She is slow in words.*

LANCE   O villain, that set this down among her vices! To 335
be slow in words is a woman's only virtue. I pray
thee, out with 't, and place it for her chief virtue.

SPEED   *Item, She is proud.*

LANCE   Out with that too; It was Eve's legacy and
cannot be ta'en from her.   340

SPEED   *Item, She hath no teeth.*

LANCE   I care not for that neither, because I love crusts.

SPEED   *Item, She is curst.*

LANCE   Well, the best is, she hath no teeth to bite.

SPEED   *Item, She will often praise her liquor.*   345

LANCE   If her liquor be good, she shall; if she will not, I
will, for good things should be praised.

SPEED   *Item, She is too liberal.*

LANCE   Of her tongue she cannot, for that's writ down
she is slow of; of her purse she shall not, for that I'll 350
keep shut; now, of another thing she may, and that
cannot I help. Well, proceed.

SPEED   *Item, She hath more hair than wit, and more*
faults than hairs, and more wealth than faults.

LANCE   Stop there. I'll have her. She was mine and not 355
mine twice or thrice in that last article. Rehearse
that once more.

SPEED   *Item, She hath more hair than wit.*

359. **prove:** test

360. **cover of the salt:** i.e., lid of the saltcellar

361. **more than the salt:** Proverbial: **"The greater hides the less"** (line 362).

367. **gracious:** acceptable

368–69. **nothing is impossible:** Proverbial: **"Nothing is impossible** to a willing heart."

371. **stays:** waits

378. **going:** walking

380. **Pox:** an exclamation of irritation

381. **swinged:** whipped

383. **after:** i.e., follow; **correction:** punishment

3.2 The Duke enlists Proteus' aid in making Sylvia fall in love with Thurio. Proteus offers to slander Valentine and to help Thurio find musicians to serenade Sylvia.

———————

1. **but that she will:** i.e., that she will not

LANCE   "More hair than wit"? It may be; I'll prove it:
the cover of the salt hides the salt, and therefore it is   360
more than the salt; the hair that covers the wit is
more than the wit, for the greater hides the less.
What's next?

SPEED   *And more faults than hairs.*

LANCE   That's monstrous! O, that that were out!   365

SPEED   *And more wealth than faults.*

LANCE   Why, that word makes the faults gracious. Well,
I'll have her, and if it be a match, as nothing is
impossible—

SPEED   What then?   370

LANCE   Why, then will I tell thee that thy master stays
for thee at the North Gate.

SPEED   For me?

LANCE   For thee? Ay, who art thou? He hath stayed for a
better man than thee.   375

SPEED   And must I go to him?

LANCE   Thou must run to him, for thou hast stayed so
long that going will scarce serve the turn.

SPEED, ⌜*handing him the paper*⌝ Why didst not tell me
sooner? Pox of your love letters!   ⌜*He exits.*⌝   380

LANCE   Now will he be swinged for reading my letter;
an unmannerly slave, that will thrust himself into
secrets. I'll after, to rejoice in the boy's correction.
⌜*He*⌝ *exits.*

Scene 2
Enter Duke ⌜*and*⌝ *Thurio.*

DUKE
Sir Thurio, fear not but that she will love you
Now Valentine is banished from her sight.

THURIO
Since his exile she hath despised me most,

5. **That:** i.e., so that

6. **This . . . impress of love:** i.e., the impression that **love** makes upon the mind; **as a figure:** i.e., like an image

7. **Trenchèd:** carved

8. **his:** its

12. **According to:** in accord with

17. **conceit:** opinion

19. **the better:** the rather, all the more ready

26. **opposes her against:** sets herself in opposition to

28. **persevers:** perseveres (accent on second syllable)

"Give me not the boots." (1.1.27)
From Jean Milles de Souvigny, *Praxis criminis
persequendi* . . . (1541).

Forsworn my company and railed at me,
That I am desperate of obtaining her.   5
DUKE
This weak impress of love is as a figure
Trenchèd in ice, which with an hour's heat
Dissolves to water and doth lose his form.
A little time will melt her frozen thoughts,
And worthless Valentine shall be forgot.   10

⌜*Enter*⌝ *Proteus.*

How now, Sir Proteus? Is your countryman,
According to our proclamation, gone?
PROTEUS   Gone, my good lord.
DUKE
My daughter takes his going grievously.
PROTEUS
A little time, my lord, will kill that grief.   15
DUKE
So I believe, but Thurio thinks not so.
Proteus, the good conceit I hold of thee,
For thou hast shown some sign of good desert,
Makes me the better to confer with thee.
PROTEUS
Longer than I prove loyal to your Grace   20
Let me not live to look upon your Grace.
DUKE
Thou know'st how willingly I would effect
The match between Sir Thurio and my daughter?
PROTEUS   I do, my lord.
DUKE
And also, I think, thou art not ignorant   25
How she opposes her against my will?
PROTEUS
She did, my lord, when Valentine was here.
DUKE
Ay, and perversely she persevers so.

35. **deliver:** pronounce
36. **circumstance:** supporting details
40. **ill:** inappropriate, offensive, disagreeable; **office:** role, duty
43. **endamage:** inflict damage on
44. **office:** task; role; **indifferent:** neither good nor bad
49. **weed:** remove (as if **her love** were a **weed**)
51–53. **unwind, ravel, bottom it:** The image is of thread being unwound and then, to prevent it from becoming tangled, rewound into a skein.   **ravel:** fall into a tangled mass   **bottom it:** wind it into a skein

"She can spin." (3.1.316)
From Johann Engel, *Astrolabium . . .* (1488).

What might we do to make the girl forget
The love of Valentine, and love Sir Thurio?　　　　30
PROTEUS
The best way is to slander Valentine
With falsehood, cowardice, and poor descent,
Three things that women highly hold in hate.
DUKE
Ay, but she'll think that it is spoke in hate.
PROTEUS
Ay, if his enemy deliver it.　　　　35
Therefore it must with circumstance be spoken
By one whom she esteemeth as his friend.
DUKE
Then you must undertake to slander him.
PROTEUS
And that, my lord, I shall be loath to do.
'Tis an ill office for a gentleman,　　　　40
Especially against his very friend.
DUKE
Where your good word cannot advantage him,
Your slander never can endamage him;
Therefore the office is indifferent,
Being entreated to it by your friend.　　　　45
PROTEUS
You have prevailed, my lord. If I can do it
By aught that I can speak in his dispraise,
She shall not long continue love to him.
But say this weed her love from Valentine,
It follows not that she will love Sir Thurio.　　　　50
THURIO
Therefore, as you unwind her love from him,
Lest it should ravel and be good to none,
You must provide to bottom it on me,
Which must be done by praising me as much
As you in worth dispraise Sir Valentine.　　　　55

56. **kind:** way

59. **revolt:** alter your allegiance

60. **Upon this warrant:** on these grounds

61. **at large:** freely

62. **lumpish:** dejected

64. **temper her:** bring her into a desirable frame of mind

68. **lay lime:** an allusion to the spreading of bird-lime to capture small birds

70. **serviceable vows:** oaths expressing your readiness to serve her

76. **discover:** reveal; **integrity:** sincerity

77–80. **Orpheus' lute . . . sands:** Orpheus was a musician in Greek mythology. The power of his music over wild animals and even inanimate objects is described in lines 78–80. **sinews:** perhaps, tendons; or, perhaps, nerves **leviathans:** whales (See longer note, page 191.) **unsounded:** i.e., unmeasured (See page 122.)

83. **consort:** group of musicians

84. **Tune a deploring dump:** sing a despairing melody

87. **inherit:** obtain

DUKE
  And, Proteus, we dare trust you in this kind
  Because we know, on Valentine's report,
  You are already Love's firm votary
  And cannot soon revolt and change your mind.
  Upon this warrant shall you have access   60
  Where you with Sylvia may confer at large—
  For she is lumpish, heavy, melancholy,
  And, for your friend's sake, will be glad of you—
  Where you may temper her by your persuasion
  To hate young Valentine and love my friend.   65
PROTEUS
  As much as I can do I will effect.—
  But you, Sir Thurio, are not sharp enough.
  You must lay lime to tangle her desires
  By wailful sonnets, whose composèd rhymes
  Should be full-fraught with serviccable vows.   70
DUKE
  Ay, much is the force of heaven-bred poesy.
PROTEUS
  Say that upon the altar of her beauty
  You sacrifice your tears, your sighs, your heart.
  Write till your ink be dry, and with your tears
  Moist it again, and frame some feeling line   75
  That may discover such integrity.
  For Orpheus' lute was strung with poets' sinews,
  Whose golden touch could soften steel and stones,
  Make tigers tame, and huge leviathans
  Forsake unsounded deeps to dance on sands.   80
  After your dire-lamenting elegies,
  Visit by night your lady's chamber window
  With some sweet consort; to their instruments
  Tune a deploring dump; the night's dead silence
  Will well become such sweet complaining   85
    grievance.
  This, or else nothing, will inhorit her.

88. **discipline:** instruction
92. **sort:** choose
93. **sonnet:** short poem
94. **give the onset:** make a beginning
95. **About it:** i.e., set about it (also at line 98)
96. **wait upon:** attend
98. **pardon you:** i.e., excuse you from attending me

Orpheus. (3.2.77–80)
From Ovid, . . . *Metamorphoseon* . . . (1565).

DUKE
  This discipline shows thou hast been in love.
THURIO, ⌜*to Proteus*⌝
  And thy advice this night I'll put in practice.
  Therefore, sweet Proteus, my direction-giver,   90
  Let us into the city presently
  To sort some gentlemen well-skilled in music.
  I have a sonnet that will serve the turn
  To give the onset to thy good advice.
DUKE   About it, gentlemen.   95
PROTEUS
  We'll wait upon your Grace till after supper
  And afterward determine our proceedings.
DUKE
  Even now about it! I will pardon you.
                                                    They exit.

THE TWO
GENTLEMEN
OF VERONA

ACT 4

4.1 Valentine and Speed are captured by outlaws. Valentine agrees to become their captain.

---

1. **passenger:** traveler
2. **If:** i.e., even if
3. **Stand:** a command to halt (but with wordplay in line 4 on **sit**); **that:** that which
5. **undone:** i.e., done for, destroyed
10. **proper:** handsome
12. **crossed with:** thwarted by
14. **disfurnish:** deprive

ACT 4

Scene 1
Enter certain Outlaws.

FIRST OUTLAW
  Fellows, stand fast. I see a passenger.
SECOND OUTLAW
  If there be ten, shrink not, but down with 'em.

⌜*Enter*⌝ *Valentine* ⌜*and*⌝ *Speed.*

THIRD OUTLAW
  Stand, sir, and throw us that you have about you.
  If not, we'll make you sit, and rifle you.
SPEED, ⌜*to Valentine*⌝
  Sir, we are undone; these are the villains   5
  That all the travelers do fear so much.
VALENTINE   My friends—
FIRST OUTLAW
  That's not so, sir. We are your enemies.
SECOND OUTLAW   Peace. We'll hear him.
THIRD OUTLAW
  Ay, by my beard, will we, for he is a proper man.   10
VALENTINE
  Then know that I have little wealth to lose.
  A man I am crossed with adversity;
  My riches are these poor habiliments,
  Of which, if you should here disfurnish me,
  You take the sum and substance that I have.   15

127

22. **crooked:** perverse

23. **What:** an interjection here introducing a question

26. **rehearse:** repeat

27. **I killed a man:** Valentine's lie may be an attempt to impress the outlaws or to remain true to the rules of courtly love by concealing his love for Sylvia.

32. **such a doom:** i.e., so light a sentence

33. **Have you the tongues:** i.e., do you know foreign languages (Since **the tongues** often referred to Greek and Latin, it is possible that, in line 34, the Folio's "trauaile" means "travail" [instead of **travel**] and refers to study.)

34. **happy:** skillful

36. **bare scalp:** tonsure, shaved crown of the head; **Robin Hood's fat friar:** i.e., Friar Tuck, a follower of the legendary outlaw Robin Hood, whose exploits were sung in ballads and celebrated in May Day pageants (See page 130.)

37. **were a king:** i.e., would make a good **king**; **faction:** i.e., band

41. **villain:** scoundrel, rogue

42. **take to:** i.e., fall back on, have recourse to

SECOND OUTLAW   Whither travel you?

VALENTINE   To Verona.

FIRST OUTLAW   Whence came you?

VALENTINE   From Milan.

THIRD OUTLAW   Have you long sojourned there?   20

VALENTINE
  Some sixteen months, and longer might have stayed
  If crooked fortune had not thwarted me.

FIRST OUTLAW   What, were you banished thence?

VALENTINE   I was.

SECOND OUTLAW   For what offense?   25

VALENTINE
  For that which now torments me to rehearse;
  I killed a man, whose death I much repent,
  But yet I slew him manfully in fight
  Without false vantage or base treachery.

FIRST OUTLAW
  Why, ne'er repent it if it were done so;   30
  But were you banished for so small a fault?

VALENTINE
  I was, and held me glad of such a doom.

SECOND OUTLAW   Have you the tongues?

VALENTINE
  My youthful travel therein made me happy,
  Or else I often had been miserable.   35

THIRD OUTLAW
  By the bare scalp of Robin Hood's fat friar,
  This fellow were a king for our wild faction.

FIRST OUTLAW   We'll have him.—Sirs, a word.
                   ⌜*The Outlaws step aside to talk.*⌝

SPEED   Master, be one of them. It's an honorable kind
  of thievery.   40

VALENTINE   Peace, villain.

SECOND OUTLAW, ⌜*advancing*⌝
  Tell us this: have you anything to take to?

43. **my fortune:** what fate or destiny holds for me
46. **awful men:** i.e., **men** worthy of respect
48. **practicing:** plotting
51. **mood:** anger
53. **to the purpose:** to get to the point
58. **quality:** profession; **want:** need
60. **above the rest:** i.e., more than the other reasons; **parley to:** i.e., discuss terms with (as if in an informal military conference)
62. **To make a virtue of necessity:** proverbial
64. **consort:** fellowship (accent on second syllable)

"Robin Hood's fat friar." (4.1.36)
From Charles Grignion, Morris dancers [n.d.].

VALENTINE   Nothing but my fortune.
THIRD OUTLAW
  Know then that some of us are gentlemen,
  Such as the fury of ungoverned youth   45
  Thrust from the company of awful men.
  Myself was from Verona banishèd
  For practicing to steal away a lady,
  ⌜An⌝ heir and ⌜near⌝ allied unto the Duke.
SECOND OUTLAW
  And I from Mantua, for a gentleman   50
  Who, in my mood, I stabbed unto the heart.
FIRST OUTLAW
  And I for such like petty crimes as these.
  But to the purpose: for we cite our faults
  That they may hold excused our lawless lives,
  And partly seeing you are beautified   55
  With goodly shape, and by your own report
  A linguist, and a man of such perfection
  As we do in our quality much want—
SECOND OUTLAW
  Indeed because you are a banished man,
  Therefore, above the rest, we parley to you.   60
  Are you content to be our general,
  To make a virtue of necessity
  And live as we do in this wilderness?
THIRD OUTLAW
  What sayst thou? Wilt thou be of our consort?
  Say ay, and be the captain of us all;   65
  We'll do thee homage and be ruled by thee,
  Love thee as our commander and our king.
FIRST OUTLAW
  But if thou scorn our courtesy, thou diest.
SECOND OUTLAW
  Thou shalt not live to brag what we have offered.

72. **silly:** defenseless; **passengers:** travelers
76. **at thy dispose:** in your charge or control

4.2 Proteus serenades Sylvia, supposedly on Thurio's behalf. As Julia watches, disguised as a page, Proteus sings his love song to Sylvia, woos her, and, having been rejected by her, succeeds in getting her promise to give him her portrait.

———————

3. **color:** pretense
4. **access:** accent on second syllable; **prefer:** promote
9. **commend:** i.e., offer
10. **have been forsworn:** i.e., have perjured myself
12. **quips:** sarcastic remarks

VALENTINE

I take your offer and will live with you,⁣ 70
Provided that you do no outrages
On silly women or poor passengers.

THIRD OUTLAW

No, we detest such vile base practices.
Come, go with us; we'll bring thee to our crews
And show thee all the treasure we have got, 75
Which, with ourselves, all rest at thy dispose.

They exit.

Scene 2
Enter Proteus.

PROTEUS

Already have I been false to Valentine,
And now I must be as unjust to Thurio.
Under the color of commending him,
I have access my own love to prefer.
But Sylvia is too fair, too true, too holy 5
To be corrupted with my worthless gifts.
When I protest true loyalty to her,
She twits me with my falsehood to my friend;
When to her beauty I commend my vows,
She bids me think how I have been forsworn 10
In breaking faith with Julia, whom I loved;
And notwithstanding all her sudden quips,
The least whereof would quell a lover's hope,
Yet, spaniel-like, the more she spurns my love,
The more it grows and fawneth on her still. 15
But here comes Thurio. Now must we to her
window
And give some evening music to her ear.

19. **are you crept:** i.e., have you come stealthily (Proteus, in line 21, puns on **creep** as "crawl.")

20–21. **love / Will creep . . . where it cannot go:** proverbial   **go:** walk

27. **lustily:** heartily, vigorously

28–29. **allycholly:** i.e., melancholy

30–31. **because I cannot be merry:** Proverbial: "I am sad because I cannot be glad."

An alehouse. (2.5.7, 52)
From August Casimir Redel, *Apophtegmata symbolica* . . . [n.d.].

⌐*Enter*⌐ *Thurio* ⌐*and Musicians.*⌐

THURIO
  How now, Sir Proteus, are you crept before us?
PROTEUS
  Ay, gentle Thurio, for you know that love   20
  Will creep in service where it cannot go.
THURIO
  Ay, but I hope, sir, that you love not here.
PROTEUS
  Sir, but I do, or else I would be hence.
THURIO
  Who, Sylvia?
PROTEUS   Ay, Sylvia, for your sake.   25
THURIO
  I thank you for your own.—Now, gentlemen,
  Let's tune, and to it lustily awhile.

  ⌐*Enter*⌐ *Host* ⌐*of the inn, and*⌐ *Julia,* ⌐*disguised as a*
  page, Sebastian. They stand at a distance and talk.⌐

HOST Now, my young guest, methinks you're ally-
    cholly. I pray you, why is it?
JULIA, ⌐*as Sebastian*⌐ Marry, mine host, because I   30
    cannot be merry.
HOST Come, we'll have you merry. I'll bring you where
    you shall hear music and see the gentleman that you
    asked for.
JULIA, ⌐*as Sebastian*⌐ But shall I hear him speak?   35
HOST Ay, that you shall.
JULIA, ⌐*as Sebastian*⌐ That will be music.
HOST Hark, hark.   ⌐*Music plays.*⌐
JULIA, ⌐*as Sebastian*⌐ Is he among these?
HOST Ay. But peace; let's hear 'em.   40

41 SP. **Proteus:** The Folio does not name the singer, but lines 58–64 seem clearly to point to Proteus as the one who sings and plays the lute.

42. **swains:** lovers, wooers

48. **Love:** i.e., Cupid, the blind god of love (See below, and page 66.) **repair:** make his way, journey

50. **inhabits:** takes up his abode, settles

57. **likes:** pleases ("Sebastian's" response is the first of a series of wordplays in which words say one thing to the Host while meaning something quite different to the speaker. See, e.g., lines 58–59, **"likes me not"**; line 61, **"plays false."**)

69. **jars so:** (1) sounds so harsh; (2) hurts so badly

70. **change:** modulation, variation

71. **change:** fickleness, inconstancy

Cupid. (2.6.42)
From Francesco Petrarca, *Opera* . . . [1508].

Song.

⌈PROTEUS⌉ *Who is Sylvia? What is she,*
      That all our swains commend her?
   Holy, fair, and wise is she;
      The heaven such grace did lend her
         That she might admirèd be.   45

   Is she kind as she is fair?
      For beauty lives with kindness.
   Love doth to her eyes repair
      To help him of his blindness;
         And, being helped, inhabits there.   50

   Then to Sylvia let us sing,
      That Sylvia is excelling;
   She excels each mortal thing
      Upon the dull earth dwelling.
         To her let us garlands bring.   55

HOST How now? Are you sadder than you were before?
   How do you, man? The music likes you not.
JULIA, ⌈*as Sebastian*⌉ You mistake. The musician likes me
   not.
HOST Why, my pretty youth?   60
JULIA, ⌈*as Sebastian*⌉ He plays false, father.
HOST How, out of tune on the strings?
JULIA, ⌈*as Sebastian*⌉ Not so; but yet so false that he
   grieves my very heart-strings.
HOST You have a quick ear.   65
JULIA, ⌈*as Sebastian*⌉ Ay, I would I were deaf; it makes
   me have a slow heart.
HOST I perceive you delight not in music.
JULIA, ⌈*as Sebastian*⌉ Not a whit when it jars so.
HOST Hark, what fine change is in the music!   70
JULIA, ⌈*as Sebastian*⌉ Ay; that change is the spite.
HOST You would have them always play but one
   thing?

74. **one play but one thing:** i.e., a person perform no more than one role

75. **talk on:** i.e., speak about

78. **out of all nick:** i.e., beyond all reckoning

82. **his lady:** i.e., Proteus' **lady**

84. **parts:** departs

85. **fear not you:** i.e., don't worry

86. **drift:** scheme

90. **even:** evening

97. **will:** wish

JULIA, ⌈*as Sebastian*⌉
    I would always have one play but one thing.
    But, host, doth this Sir Proteus, that we talk on,   75
    Often resort unto this gentlewoman?
HOST   I tell you what Lance his man told me: he loved
    her out of all nick.
JULIA, ⌈*as Sebastian*⌉ Where is Lance?
HOST   Gone to seek his dog, which tomorrow, by his   80
    master's command, he must carry for a present to
    his lady.   ⌈*Music ends.*⌉
JULIA, ⌈*as Sebastian*⌉ Peace. Stand aside. The company
    parts.   ⌈*Host and Julia move away.*⌉
PROTEUS
    Sir Thurio, fear not you. I will so plead   85
    That you shall say my cunning drift excels.
THURIO
    Where meet we?
PROTEUS   At Saint Gregory's well.
THURIO   Farewell.
           ⌈*Thurio and the Musicians exit.*⌉

        ⌈*Enter*⌉ Sylvia, ⌈*above.*⌉

PROTEUS
    Madam, good even to your Ladyship.   90
SYLVIA
    I thank you for your music, gentlemen.
    Who is that that spake?
PROTEUS
    One, lady, if you knew his pure heart's truth,
    You would quickly learn to know him by his voice.
SYLVIA   Sir Proteus, as I take it.   95
PROTEUS
    Sir Proteus, gentle lady, and your servant.
SYLVIA
    What's your will?

98. **compass yours:** obtain your **will** (i.e., your consent; your sexual desire)

100. **presently:** immediately

101. **subtle:** treacherously cunning

102. **conceitless:** devoid of understanding

106. **For:** i.e., as for; **this pale queen of night:** i.e., the moon, personified as Diana, goddess of chastity (See below.)

108. **suit:** courting

113. **if I:** i.e., even if I (who am no longer Julia)

118. **importunacy:** troublesome pertinacity

123. **hers:** i.e., her love

124. **hers:** i.e., her **grave; sepulcher:** inter (accent on second syllable)

"This pale queen of night." (4.2.106)
From Robert Whitcombe, *Janua divorum* . . . (1678).

PROTEUS   That I may compass yours.
SYLVIA
  You have your wish: my will is even this,
  That presently you hie you home to bed.   100
  Thou subtle, perjured, false, disloyal man,
  Think'st thou I am so shallow, so conceitless,
  To be seducèd by thy flattery,
  That hast deceived so many with thy vows?
  Return, return, and make thy love amends.   105
  For me, by this pale queen of night I swear,
  I am so far from granting thy request
  That I despise thee for thy wrongful suit
  And by and by intend to chide myself
  Even for this time I spend in talking to thee.   110
PROTEUS
  I grant, sweet love, that I did love a lady,
  But she is dead.
JULIA, ⌜*aside*⌝   'Twere false if I should speak it,
  For I am sure she is not burièd.
SYLVIA
  Say that she be; yet Valentine thy friend   115
  Survives, to whom, thyself art witness,
  I am betrothed. And art thou not ashamed
  To wrong him with thy importunacy?
PROTEUS
  I likewise hear that Valentine is dead.
SYLVIA
  And so suppose am I, for in ⌜his⌝ grave,   120
  Assure thyself, my love is burièd.
PROTEUS
  Sweet lady, let me rake it from the earth.
SYLVIA
  Go to thy lady's grave and call hers thence,
  Or, at the least, in hers sepulcher thine.
JULIA, ⌜*aside*⌝ He heard not that.   125

130. **substance:** Wordplay in lines 130–37 turns on meanings of **substance** and its opposite, **shadow**. Here, **substance** is "essential part." In line 133 it is a "solid or real thing." **Shadow** means, variously, "insubstantial form," "portrait," "actor," and "illusion."

131. **else:** elsewhere

143. **By my halidom:** a mild oath (**Halidom** referred vaguely to relics and other sacred things.)

144. **lies:** lodges

148. **watched:** stayed awake; **most heaviest:** most sorrowful, distressful, or grievous (**Heaviest** could also mean simply "sleepiest" or "weariest.")

4.3 Sylvia, determined to escape the pursuit of Thurio and Proteus, persuades Sir Eglamour to accompany her that evening on a journey to find Valentine.

PROTEUS
  Madam, if your heart be so obdurate,
  Vouchsafe me yet your picture for my love,
  The picture that is hanging in your chamber;
  To that I'll speak, to that I'll sigh and weep,
  For since the substance of your perfect self   130
  Is else devoted, I am but a shadow;
  And to your shadow will I make true love.
JULIA, ⌈*aside*⌉
  If 'twere a substance you would sure deceive it
  And make it but a shadow, as I am.
SYLVIA
  I am very loath to be your idol, sir;   135
  But since your falsehood shall become you well
  To worship shadows and adore false shapes,
  Send to me in the morning, and I'll send it.
  And so, good rest.   ⌈*Sylvia exits.*⌉
PROTEUS   As wretches have o'ernight   140
  That wait for execution in the morn. ⌈*Proteus exits.*⌉
JULIA, ⌈*as Sebastian*⌉ Host, will you go?
HOST   By my halidom, I was fast asleep.
JULIA, ⌈*as Sebastian*⌉ Pray you, where lies Sir Proteus?
HOST   Marry, at my house. Trust me, I think 'tis almost 145
  day.
JULIA, ⌈*as Sebastian*⌉
  Not so; but it hath been the longest night
  That e'er I watched, and the most heaviest.
                        ⌈*They exit.*⌉

Scene 3
Enter Eglamour.

EGLAMOUR
  This is the hour that Madam Sylvia
  Entreated me to call and know her mind;

7. **attends:** awaits

10. **impose:** charge, command

15. **remorseful:** full of pity

16. **dear:** affectionate, loving

19. **abhorred:** The past tense is thought by some to be a printing-house error, and by others to mean "would have **abhorred** as a husband."

24. **would:** i.e., wish to go

25. **makes abode:** i.e., dwells

26. **for:** because; **ways:** roads; **pass:** travel

28. **repose:** rely

29. **Urge not:** i.e., don't bring up (your concerns about)

31. **justice:** justness, propriety, correctness

There's some great matter she'd employ me in.
Madam, madam!

⌜*Enter*⌝ *Sylvia,* ⌜*above.*⌝

SYLVIA   Who calls?   5
EGLAMOUR   Your servant, and your friend,
One that attends your Ladyship's command.
SYLVIA
Sir Eglamour, a thousand times good morrow.
EGLAMOUR
As many, worthy lady, to yourself.
According to your Ladyship's impose,   10
I am thus early come to know what service
It is your pleasure to command me in.
SYLVIA
O Eglamour, thou art a gentleman—
Think not I flatter, for I swear I do not—
Valiant, wise, remorseful, well accomplished.   15
Thou art not ignorant what dear good will
I bear unto the banished Valentine,
Nor how my father would enforce me marry
Vain Thurio, whom my very soul abhorred.
Thyself hast loved, and I have heard thee say   20
No grief did ever come so near thy heart
As when thy lady and thy true love died,
Upon whose grave thou vow'dst pure chastity.
Sir Eglamour, I would to Valentine,
To Mantua, where I hear he makes abode;   25
And for the ways are dangerous to pass,
I do desire thy worthy company,
Upon whose faith and honor I repose.
Urge not my father's anger, Eglamour,
But think upon my grief, a lady's grief,   30
And on the justice of my flying hence

33. **still rewards:** i.e., always reward

39. **grievances:** oppressive circumstances

40. **they virtuously are placed:** perhaps, they are not caused by any improper behavior on your part

42. **Recking:** caring; **what betideth:** what happens to

43. **As much:** i.e., as much as; **befortune:** to befall

4.4 Proteus learns to his horror that Lance has tried to present Crab to Sylvia as a gift. Proteus then sends Sebastian (Julia in disguise) to Sylvia with a letter and a ring. Sylvia refuses these gifts, but sends Proteus the promised picture of herself.

———————

3. **of:** from

4. **blind:** i.e., newborn (before the eyes are open)

4–5. **went to it:** i.e., were drowned

To keep me from a most unholy match,
Which heaven and fortune still rewards with plagues.
I do desire thee, even from a heart
As full of sorrows as the sea of sands,   35
To bear me company and go with me;
If not, to hide what I have said to thee,
That I may venture to depart alone.

EGLAMOUR
Madam, I pity much your grievances,
Which, since I know they virtuously are placed,   40
I give consent to go along with you,
⌜Recking⌝ as little what betideth me
As much I wish all good befortune you.
When will you go?

SYLVIA   This evening coming.   45

EGLAMOUR
Where shall I meet you?

SYLVIA   At Friar Patrick's cell,
Where I intend holy confession.

EGLAMOUR
I will not fail your Ladyship. Good morrow, gentle
   lady.   50

SYLVIA
Good morrow, kind Sir Eglamour.

                                        They exit.

                        Scene 4
            Enter Lance, ⌜with his dog, Crab.⌝

LANCE When a man's servant shall play the cur with
   him, look you, it goes hard—one that I brought up
   of a puppy, one that I saved from drowning when
   three or four of his blind brothers and sisters went
   to it. I have taught him even as one would say   5
   precisely "Thus I would teach a dog." I was sent to

9. **steps me:** i.e., steps

11. **keep:** restrain

12. **takes upon him:** undertakes

13. **be . . . a dog at:** proverbial for "be adept at"

14–15. **to take . . . he did:** i.e., to take the blame for an offense that he made

15. **hanged:** Dogs were actually **hanged** for offenses in this period.

17. **thrusts me:** i.e., thrusts

19. **bless the mark:** a phrase used to ask pardon for offensive language

19–20. **a pissing while:** proverbial for "a short time," but here also meant literally

22–23. **Hang him up:** i.e., hang him

24. **goes me:** i.e., I went

28. **wot of:** are aware of; **makes me:** i.e., makes

31. **stocks:** an instrument of punishment that imprisoned the legs in a wooden frame (See page 152.) **puddings:** boiled sausages

33. **pillory:** a contraption much like the **stocks,** except that the head and hands were imprisoned in the frame

36. **served:** played; **took my leave of:** was bidding farewell to

37. **bid thee still mark me:** order you always to pay attention to me

38–39. **make water:** urinate

deliver him as a present to Mistress Sylvia from my
master; and I came no sooner into the dining
chamber but he steps me to her trencher and steals
her capon's leg. O, 'tis a foul thing when a cur   10
cannot keep himself in all companies! I would have,
as one should say, one that takes upon him to be a
dog indeed; to be, as it were, a dog at all things. If I
had not had more wit than he, to take a fault upon
me that he did, I think verily he had been hanged   15
for 't. Sure as I live, he had suffered for 't. You shall
judge. He thrusts me himself into the company of
three or four gentlemanlike dogs under the Duke's
table; he had not been there—bless the mark!—a
pissing while but all the chamber smelt him. "Out   20
with the dog!" says one. "What cur is that?" says
another. "Whip him out!" says the third. "Hang him
up!" says the Duke. I, having been acquainted with
the smell before, knew it was Crab, and goes me to
the fellow that whips the dogs. "Friend," quoth I,   25
"You mean to whip the dog?" "Ay, marry, do I,"
quoth he. "You do him the more wrong," quoth I.
" 'Twas I did the thing you wot of." He makes me no
more ado but whips me out of the chamber. How
many masters would do this for his servant? Nay,   30
I'll be sworn I have sat in the stocks for puddings he
hath stolen; otherwise he had been executed. I have
stood on the pillory for geese he hath killed; otherwise he had suffered for 't. ⌜*To Crab.*⌝ Thou think'st
not of this now. Nay, I remember the trick you   35
served me when I took my leave of Madam Sylvia.
Did not I bid thee still mark me, and do as I do?
When didst thou see me heave up my leg and make
water against a gentlewoman's farthingale? Didst
thou ever see me do such a trick?   40

45. **whoreson:** sometimes used as a term of jocular familiarity

56. **this:** i.e., Crab

57. **squirrel:** i.e., tiny lap dog (In Shakespeare's time, actual squirrels were also kept as pets.)

64. **slave:** rascal; **still an end:** constantly; **turns me to shame:** brings me into disgrace

65. **entertainèd thee:** i.e., taken you into my service

A dog in "the dining chamber." (4.4.5–10)
From T[homas] F[ella], *A book of diverse devices . . .* (1585–1622).

⌜*Enter*⌝ *Proteus* ⌜*and*⌝ *Julia* ⌜*disguised as Sebastian.*⌝

PROTEUS
  Sebastian is thy name? I like thee well
  And will employ thee in some service presently.
JULIA, ⌜*as Sebastian*⌝
  In what you please. I'll do what I can.
PROTEUS
  I hope thou wilt. ⌜*To Lance.*⌝ How now, you
    whoreson peasant?   45
  Where have you been these two days loitering?
LANCE Marry, sir, I carried Mistress Sylvia the dog you
    bade me.
PROTEUS And what says she to my little jewel?
LANCE Marry, she says your dog was a cur, and tells   50
    you currish thanks is good enough for such a
    present.
PROTEUS But she received my dog?
LANCE No, indeed, did she not. Here have I brought
    him back again.   55
PROTEUS What, didst thou offer her this from me?
LANCE Ay, sir. The other squirrel was stolen from me
    by the hangman's boys in the market-place, and
    then I offered her mine own, who is a dog as big as
    ten of yours, and therefore the gift the greater.   60
PROTEUS
  Go, get thee hence, and find my dog again,
  Or ne'er return again into my sight.
  Away, I say. Stayest thou to vex me here?
                          ⌜*Lance exits with Crab.*⌝
  A slave that still an end turns me to shame.
  Sebastian, I have entertainèd thee,   65
  Partly that I have need of such a youth
  That can with some discretion do my business—
  For 'tis no trusting to yond foolish lout—
  But chiefly for thy face and thy behavior,

73. **presently:** immediately
75. **delivered:** who gave
76. **leave:** abandon
77. **belike:** perhaps
82. **Wherefore:** why
83. **methinks:** it seems to me
89. **therewithal:** with it
93. **hie:** hurry
96–97. **thou hast . . . lambs:** Proverbial: "Do not let the wolf guard the sheep." (Shakespeare standardly changes "wolf" to "fox" in his use of the proverb.)
98. **poor fool:** addressed to herself

"I have sat in the stocks." (4.4.31)
From T[homas] F[ella], *A book of diverse devices* . . . (1585–1622).

Which, if my augury deceive me not,   70
Witness good bringing-up, fortune, and truth.
Therefore, know ⌜thou,⌝ for this I entertain thee.
Go presently, and take this ring with thee;
Deliver it to Madam Sylvia.
She loved me well delivered it to me.   75
                              ⌜*He gives her a ring.*⌝

JULIA, ⌜*as Sebastian*⌝
  It seems you loved not her, ⌜to⌝ leave her token.
  She is dead belike?

PROTEUS   Not so; I think she lives.

JULIA, ⌜*as Sebastian*⌝ Alas!

PROTEUS   Why dost thou cry "Alas"?   80

JULIA, ⌜*as Sebastian*⌝   I cannot choose but pity her.

PROTEUS   Wherefore shouldst thou pity her?

JULIA, ⌜*as Sebastian*⌝
  Because methinks that she loved you as well
  As you do love your lady Sylvia.
  She dreams on him that has forgot her love;   85
  You dote on her that cares not for your love.
  'Tis pity love should be so contrary,
  And thinking on it makes me cry "Alas."

PROTEUS
  Well, give her that ring and therewithal
  This letter. ⌜*He gives her a paper.*⌝ That's her   90
    chamber. Tell my lady
  I claim the promise for her heavenly picture.
  Your message done, hie home unto my chamber,
  Where thou shalt find me sad and solitary.
                              ⌜*Proteus exits.*⌝

JULIA
  How many women would do such a message?   95
  Alas, poor Proteus, thou hast entertained
  A fox to be the shepherd of thy lambs.
  Alas, poor fool, why do I pity him

106, 107. **would have:** i.e., wish to have
113. **speed:** succeed
115. **mean:** intermediary, agent
117. **would you:** i.e., do you wish
128. **shadow:** picture

A "sun-expelling mask." (4.4.162)
From Cesare Vecellio, *Degli habiti antichi et moderni . . .* (1590).

That with his very heart despiseth me?
Because he loves her, he despiseth me;　　　　　100
Because I love him, I must pity him.
This ring I gave him when he parted from me,
To bind him to remember my good will;
And now am I, unhappy messenger,
To plead for that which I would not obtain,　　　105
To carry that which I would have refused,
To praise his faith, which I would have dispraised.
I am my master's true confirmèd love,
But cannot be true servant to my master
Unless I prove false traitor to myself.　　　　110
Yet will I woo for him, but yet so coldly
As—Heaven it knows!—I would not have him
　speed.

⌜*Enter*⌝ *Sylvia.*

⌜*As Sebastian*⌝ Gentlewoman, good day. I pray you be
　my mean　　　　　　　　　　　　　　　115
To bring me where to speak with Madam Sylvia.
SYLVIA
What would you with her, if that I be she?
JULIA, ⌜*as Sebastian*⌝
If you be she, I do entreat your patience
To hear me speak the message I am sent on.
SYLVIA　From whom?　　　　　　　　　　120
JULIA, ⌜*as Sebastian*⌝ From my master, Sir Proteus,
　madam.
SYLVIA　O, he sends you for a picture?
JULIA, ⌜*as Sebastian*⌝ Ay, madam.
SYLVIA, ⌜*calling*⌝ Ursula, bring my picture there.　　125
　　　　　　　⌜*She is brought the picture.*⌝
Go, give your master this. Tell him from me,
One Julia, that his changing thoughts forget,
Would better fit his chamber than this shadow.

131. **unadvised:** carelessly, inadvertently

136. **There, hold:** Sylvia may well try to return the letter to Julia with this line.

139. **new-found:** newly invented

149. **tender her:** regard her with pity

Love, "a blinded god." (4.4.206)
From Guillaume de la Perrière, *Le théâtre des bons engins* . . . (1539).

JULIA, ⌜*as Sebastian*⌝ Madam, please you peruse this
    letter.   ⌜*She gives Sylvia a paper.*⌝ 130
  Pardon me, madam, I have unadvised
  Delivered you a paper that I should not.
  This is the letter to your Ladyship.
                    ⌜*She takes back the first paper
                    and hands Sylvia another.*⌝

SYLVIA
  I pray thee let me look on that again.
JULIA, ⌜*as Sebastian*⌝
  It may not be; good madam, pardon me.   135
SYLVIA There, hold.
  I will not look upon your master's lines;
  I know they are stuffed with protestations
  And full of new-found oaths, which he will break
  As easily as I do tear his paper.   140
                    ⌜*She tears the second paper.*⌝

JULIA, ⌜*as Sebastian*⌝
  Madam, he sends your Ladyship this ring.
                    ⌜*She offers Sylvia a ring*⌝

SYLVIA
  The more shame for him, that he sends it me;
  For I have heard him say a thousand times
  His Julia gave it him at his departure.
  Though his false finger have profaned the ring,   145
  Mine shall not do his Julia so much wrong.
JULIA, ⌜*as Sebastian*⌝ She thanks you.
SYLVIA What sayst thou?
JULIA, ⌜*as Sebastian*⌝
  I thank you, madam, that you tender her;
  Poor gentlewoman, my master wrongs her much.   150
SYLVIA Dost thou know her?
JULIA, ⌜*as Sebastian*⌝
  Almost as well as I do know myself.

154. **several:** separate

157. **passing:** surpassingly, extremely; **fair:** beautiful (In her response, Julia sometimes plays on **fair** as light-skinned.)

162. **sun-expelling mask:** The reference is to women's use of masks to protect the skin from the sun. (See page 154.)

163. **starved:** destroyed

164. **pinched:** caused to shrivel or wither up (This meaning was used in reference to plants, so that here the **lily tincture** [i.e., skin the color of the **lily**] becomes the actual **lily** that has withered.)

165. **black:** i.e., tanned (Editors suggest that she also means "ugly," but lines 195–96 contradict that meaning.)

167. **Pentecost:** Whitsuntide, the seventh week after Easter

168. **pageants of delight:** i.e., delightful entertainments

169. **play the woman's part:** This reference to the custom of boys playing women's parts on the Elizabethan stage is particularly rich, in that it would have been delivered by a boy actor playing a girl who is playing a boy who is "remembering" playing a girl in a Whitsun play.

170. **trimmed:** dressed

174. **agood:** heartily

176–77. **Ariadne . . . flight:** In Greek mythology, **Ariadne** saves Theseus and is then abandoned by him. **passioning:** sorrowing

179. **therewithal:** i.e., by the performance (literally, "with that")

182. **beholding:** beholden

To think upon her woes, I do protest
That I have wept a hundred several times.

SYLVIA
Belike she thinks that Proteus hath forsook her?   155

JULIA, ⸤*as Sebastian*⸥
I think she doth, and that's her cause of sorrow.

SYLVIA   Is she not passing fair?

JULIA, ⸤*as Sebastian*⸥
She hath been fairer, madam, than she is;
When she did think my master loved her well,
She, in my judgment, was as fair as you.   160
But since she did neglect her looking-glass
And threw her sun-expelling mask away,
The air hath starved the roses in her cheeks
And pinched the lily tincture of her face,
That now she is become as black as I.   165

SYLVIA   How tall was she?

JULIA, ⸤*as Sebastian*⸥
About my stature; for at Pentecost,
When all our pageants of delight were played,
Our youth got me to play the woman's part,
And I was trimmed in Madam Julia's gown,   170
Which served me as fit, by all men's judgments,
As if the garment had been made for me;
Therefore I know she is about my height.
And at that time I made her weep agood,
For I did play a lamentable part;   175
Madam, 'twas Ariadne, passioning
For Theseus' perjury and unjust flight,
Which I so lively acted with my tears
That my poor mistress, movèd therewithal,
Wept bitterly; and would I might be dead   180
If I in thought felt not her very sorrow.

SYLVIA
She is beholding to thee, gentle youth.

191. **but cold:** i.e., unpersuasive

192. **my mistress':** Note that Julia continues to speak as Sebastian, even though she is alone onstage. Beginning with line 193, she speaks as herself.

195. **tire:** headdress

198. **flatter with myself:** (1) compliment myself unduly; (2) encourage myself with false hopes

199. **auburn:** blond (The meaning of the word changed in later centuries.)

201. **such a colored periwig:** i.e., a wig of that color

203. **mine's as high:** It is unclear whether Julia means that her forehead is no higher than Sylvia's or that it is **as high** as Sylvia's is **low.** (High foreheads were admired.)

205. **But I can make respective:** i.e., that I cannot make worthy of respect

206. **a blinded god:** Because, proverbially, "love is blind," Cupid is presented as blindfolded or **blinded.** (See pages 44, 66, 156.)

207. **shadow:** For the various senses of **shadow** and **substance** in lines 207–12, see note to 4.2.130.

208. **'tis thy rival:** playing on **take ... up** (line 207) as both "pick up" and "oppose"; **senseless:** insensate

211. **sense:** reason

212. **statue:** i.e., an object of **idolatry**

Alas, poor lady, desolate and left!
I weep myself to think upon thy words.
Here, youth, there is my purse.   185
⌜*She gives Julia a purse.*⌝
                    I give thee this
For thy sweet mistress' sake, because thou lov'st her.
Farewell.

JULIA, ⌜*as Sebastian*⌝
And she shall thank you for 't if e'er you know her.
                    ⌜*Sylvia exits.*⌝

A virtuous gentlewoman, mild and beautiful.   190
I hope my master's suit will be but cold,
Since she respects my mistress' love so much.—
Alas, how love can trifle with itself!
Here is her picture; let me see. I think
If I had such a tire, this face of mine   195
Were full as lovely as is this of hers;
And yet the painter flattered her a little,
Unless I flatter with myself too much.
Her hair is auburn; mine is perfect yellow;
If that be all the difference in his love,   200
I'll get me such a colored periwig.
Her eyes are gray as glass, and so are mine.
Ay, but her forehead's low, and mine's as high.
What should it be that he respects in her
But I can make respective in myself   205
If this fond Love were not a blinded god?
Come, shadow, come, and take this shadow up,
For 'tis thy rival. O, thou senseless form,
Thou shalt be worshipped, kissed, loved, and
      adored;   210
And were there sense in his idolatry,
My substance should be statue in thy stead.

214. Jove: king of the gods in Roman mythology (See below.)

Jove. (4.4.214)
From Vincenzo Cartari, *Le vere e noue imagini . . .* (1615).

I'll use thee kindly for thy mistress' sake,
That used me so, or else, by Jove I vow,
I should have scratched out your unseeing eyes   215
To make my master out of love with thee.

⌜*She*⌝ *exits.*

THE TWO GENTLEMEN OF VERONA

ACT 5

5.1 Sylvia and Sir Eglamour set out on their journey.

———————

4. **break not hours:** i.e., do not fail to meet their appointed time
6. **spur their expedition:** Proverbial: "He that has love in his breast has spurs at his sides."
10. **attended:** watched over
12. **recover:** reach; **sure:** safe

"A robin redbreast." (2.1.20–21)
From Konrad Gesner, . . . *Historiae animalium* . . . (1585–1604).

ACT 5

Scene 1
Enter Eglamour.

EGLAMOUR
  The sun begins to gild the western sky,
  And now it is about the very hour
  That Sylvia at Friar Patrick's cell should meet me.
  She will not fail, for lovers break not hours,
  Unless it be to come before their time,   5
  So much they spur their expedition.

          ⌜*Enter*⌝ *Sylvia.*

  See where she comes.—Lady, a happy evening.
SYLVIA
  Amen, amen. Go on, good Eglamour,
  Out at the postern by the abbey wall.
  I fear I am attended by some spies.   10
EGLAMOUR
  Fear not. The forest is not three leagues off;
  If we recover that, we are sure enough.
                      They exit.

5.2 The Duke informs Proteus and Thurio of Sylvia's flight. They each decide to follow her.

---

3. **takes exceptions at:** i.e., objects to; **person:** bodily frame or figure

5. **little:** i.e., thin

7. **spurred:** wordplay on **boot** (line 6) as a riding boot with spurs

8. **to:** about

9. **fair:** nice-looking or fair-skinned (To be "fair-faced" also meant to be **fair** to the eye only, or to be specious.)

10. **wanton:** rogue, trifler; **black:** swarthy

12. **Black . . . eyes:** proverbial **pearls:** precious objects (but used by Julia in line 13 to mean "cataracts")

14. **wink:** i.e., close my eyes

15. **discourse:** conversation

16. **Ill:** badly

20. **makes no doubt of:** i.e., has no doubts about

Scene 2

Enter Thurio, Proteus, ⌈and⌉ Julia, ⌈disguised as
Sebastian.⌉

THURIO
  Sir Proteus, what says Sylvia to my suit?
PROTEUS
  O sir, I find her milder than she was,
  And yet she takes exceptions at your person.
THURIO   What? That my leg is too long?
PROTEUS   No, that it is too little.   5
THURIO
  I'll wear a boot to make it somewhat rounder.
⌈JULIA, *aside*⌉
  But love will not be spurred to what it loathes.
THURIO   What says she to my face?
PROTEUS   She says it is a fair one.
THURIO
  Nay, then the wanton lies; my face is black.   10
PROTEUS
  But pearls are fair, and the old saying is,
  Black men are pearls in beauteous ladies' eyes.
⌈JULIA, *aside*⌉
  'Tis true, such pearls as put out ladies' eyes,
  For I had rather wink than look on them.
THURIO   How likes she my discourse?   15
PROTEUS   Ill, when you talk of war.
THURIO
  But well when I discourse of love and peace.
JULIA, ⌈*aside*⌉
  But better, indeed, when you hold ⌈your⌉ peace.
THURIO   What says she to my valor?
PROTEUS   O, sir, she makes no doubt of that.   20
JULIA, ⌈*aside*⌉
  She needs not when she knows it cowardice.

23. **well derived:** descended from good ancestors (but used by Julia in line 24 as if his was a descent from gentlemanly status to that of **a fool**)

25. **possessions:** properties

27. **Wherefore:** why

28. **owe:** own

29. **out by lease:** i.e., leased out to others

37. **peasant:** here, a term of abuse

42. **being masked:** i.e., since she was wearing a mask (See note to 4.4.162.)

44. **even:** evening

45. **likelihoods:** indications, signs

46. **stand not to discourse:** i.e., do not delay in order to talk (about it)

48. **Upon . . . foot:** i.e., on the upward slope of the foot of the mountain

50. **Dispatch:** make haste

A Franciscan friar. (4.3.47, 5.1.3)
From Niccolo Catalano, *Fiume del terrestre paradiso* . . . (1652).

THURIO   What says she to my birth?
PROTEUS   That you are well derived.
JULIA, ⌜*aside*⌝ True, from a gentleman to a fool.
THURIO   Considers she my possessions?   25
PROTEUS   O, ay, and pities them.
THURIO   Wherefore?
JULIA, ⌜*aside*⌝ That such an ass should owe them.
PROTEUS
   That they are out by lease.
JULIA, ⌜*as Sebastian*⌝   Here comes the Duke.   30

⌜*Enter*⌝ *Duke.*

DUKE
   How now, Sir Proteus?—How now, Thurio?
   Which of you saw Eglamour of late?
THURIO
   Not I.
PROTEUS Nor I.
DUKE   Saw you my daughter?   35
PROTEUS   Neither.
DUKE
   Why, then, she's fled unto that peasant, Valentine,
   And Eglamour is in her company.
   'Tis true, for Friar Lawrence met them both
   As he, in penance, wandered through the forest;   40
   Him he knew well and guessed that it was she,
   But, being masked, he was not sure of it.
   Besides, she did intend confession
   At Patrick's cell this even, and there she was not.
   These likelihoods confirm her flight from hence.   45
   Therefore I pray you stand not to discourse,
   But mount you presently and meet with me
   Upon the rising of the mountain foot
   That leads toward Mantua, whither they are fled.
   Dispatch, sweet gentlemen, and follow me.   50
                                         ⌜*He exits.*⌝

51. **peevish:** obstinate
54. **reckless:** inconsiderate
57. **cross:** thwart
58. **that is gone for:** i.e., who has fled for the sake of

5.3 Sylvia is captured by the outlaws, while Sir Eglamour flees.

———————

4. **learned:** taught
11. **beset:** surrounded

A shepherd with his sheep. (1.1.76–77)
From *Hortus sanitatis* . . . (1536).

THURIO
  Why, this it is to be a peevish girl
  That flies her fortune when it follows her.
  I'll after, more to be revenged on Eglamour
  Than for the love of reckless Sylvia.   ⌜*He exits.*⌝
PROTEUS
  And I will follow, more for Sylvia's love   55
  Than hate of Eglamour that goes with her.
                                          ⌜*He exits.*⌝
JULIA
  And I will follow, more to cross that love
  Than hate for Sylvia, that is gone for love.
                                          ⌜*She*⌝ *exits.*

Scene 3
⌜*Enter*⌝ *Sylvia* ⌜*and*⌝ *Outlaws*

FIRST OUTLAW
  Come, come, be patient. We must bring you to our
    captain.
SYLVIA
  A thousand more mischances than this one
  Have learned me how to brook this patiently.
SECOND OUTLAW   Come, bring her away.   5
FIRST OUTLAW
  Where is the gentleman that was with her?
THIRD OUTLAW
  Being nimble-footed, he hath outrun us,
  But Moyses and Valerius follow him.
  Go thou with her to the west end of the wood;
  There is our captain. We'll follow him that's fled.   10
  The thicket is beset; he cannot 'scape.
                      ⌜*Second and Third Outlaws exit.*⌝
FIRST OUTLAW
  Come, I must bring you to our captain's cave.

5.4 As Valentine watches from hiding, Sylvia is brought in by Proteus, who has taken her from the outlaws. Proteus pleads for Sylvia's love, and when she refuses him he tries to rape her. Valentine prevents the rape, listens to Proteus' speech of repentance, and, as a gesture of his friendship, offers his rights in Sylvia to Proteus. Julia faints. On recovering, she reveals herself and accuses Proteus of inconstancy. He again repents, and Julia accepts his protestations of love. The outlaws bring in the Duke and Thurio. When Thurio refuses to fight for Sylvia, the Duke accepts Valentine as a son-in-law.

———————

1. **use:** custom; **habit:** settled practice
2. **desert:** uninhabited forest
3. **better brook:** i.e., put up with more easily
6. **record:** sing
7. **inhabit:** dwell (Lines 7–10 are addressed to his heart, which has been left with Sylvia.)
8. **mansion:** dwelling place
9. **ruinous:** decayed, dilapidated
12. **cherish:** comfort
13. **hallowing:** shouting
14. **mates:** comrades, fellows
15. **Have . . . in chase:** i.e., who are pursuing some unlucky traveler

Fear not; he bears an honorable mind
And will not use a woman lawlessly.

SYLVIA
O Valentine, this I endure for thcc!   15

They exit.

Scene 4
Enter Valentine.

VALENTINE
How use doth breed a habit in a man!
This shadowy desert, unfrequented woods,
I better brook than flourishing peopled towns;
Here can I sit alone, unseen of any,
And to the nightingale's complaining notes   5
Tune my distresses and record my woes.
O thou that dost inhabit in my breast,
Leave not the mansion so long tenantless
Lest, growing ruinous, the building fall
And leave no memory of what it was.   10
Repair me with thy presence, Sylvia;
Thou gentle nymph, cherish thy forlorn swain.
              ⌜*Shouting and sounds of fighting.*⌝
What hallowing and what stir is this today?
These are my mates, that make their wills their law,
Have some unhappy passenger in chase.   15
They love me well, yet I have much to do
To keep them from uncivil outrages.
Withdraw thee, Valentine. Who's this comes here?
                          ⌜*He steps aside.*⌝

⌜*Enter*⌝ Proteus, Sylvia, ⌜*and*⌝ Julia, ⌜*disguised as*
Sebastian.⌝

PROTEUS
Madam, this service I have done for you—

20. **respect not:** have no regard for
23. **meed:** reward
37. **tender:** precious
38. **full:** entirely
41. **stood it:** i.e., even if it stood
43. **still:** always, invariably; **approved:** confirmed by experience

Though you respect not aught your servant doth—   20
To hazard life, and rescue you from him
That would have forced your honor and your love.
Vouchsafe me for my meed but one fair look;
A smaller boon than this I cannot beg,
And less than this I am sure you cannot give.   25

VALENTINE, ⌜*aside*⌝
How like a dream is this I see and hear!
Love, lend me patience to forbear awhile.

SYLVIA
O miserable, unhappy that I am!

PROTEUS
Unhappy were you, madam, ere I came,
But by my coming, I have made you happy.   30

SYLVIA
By thy approach thou mak'st me most unhappy.

JULIA, ⌜*aside*⌝
And me, when he approacheth to your presence.

SYLVIA
Had I been seizèd by a hungry lion,
I would have been a breakfast to the beast
Rather than have false Proteus rescue me.   35
O heaven, be judge how I love Valentine,
Whose life's as tender to me as my soul;
And full as much, for more there cannot be,
I do detest false perjured Proteus.
Therefore begone; solicit me no more.   40

PROTEUS
What dangerous action, stood it next to death,
Would I not undergo for one calm look!
O, 'tis the curse in love, and still approved,
When women cannot love where they're beloved.

SYLVIA
When Proteus cannot love where he's beloved.   45
Read over Julia's heart, thy first best love,
For whose dear sake thou didst then rend thy faith

49. **Descended into perjury:** i.e., forswore, perjured (**Descended** here means, literally, "caused to descend.")

50. **faith:** fidelity, loyalty; **unless thou'dst two:** i.e., unless you have loyalties to two women

53. **counterfeit to:** i.e., deceiver of

54–55. **In love / Who respects friend:** proverbial **respects:** considers

57. **moving words:** i.e., language that touches the feelings

59. **at arms' end:** i.e., at the end of my sword

64. **friend of an ill fashion:** i.e., hostile or unfriendly kind of **friend**

66. **common:** ordinary, inferior (The phrase may be modeled on the familiar "common criminal" or "common nuisance.") **faith:** loyalty

68. **beguiled:** disappointed

74. **for thy sake:** i.e., because of you

75. **private wound:** i.e., **wound** given one by a friend

Into a thousand oaths; and all those oaths
Descended into perjury to love me.
Thou hast no faith left now unless thou'dst two,   50
And that's far worse than none; better have none
Than plural faith, which is too much by one.
Thou counterfeit to thy true friend!

PROTEUS   In love
Who respects friend?   55

SYLVIA   All men but Proteus.

PROTEUS
Nay, if the gentle spirit of moving words
Can no way change you to a milder form,
I'll woo you like a soldier, at arms' end,
And love you 'gainst the nature of love—force you.   60
                            ⌜*He seizes her.*⌝

SYLVIA
O, heaven!

PROTEUS   I'll force thee yield to my desire.

VALENTINE, ⌜*advancing*⌝
Ruffian, let go that rude uncivil touch,
Thou friend of an ill fashion.

PROTEUS   Valentine!   65

VALENTINE
Thou common friend, that's without faith or love,
For such is a friend now. Treacherous man,
Thou hast beguiled my hopes; nought but mine eye
Could have persuaded me. Now I dare not say
I have one friend alive; thou wouldst disprove me.   70
Who should be trusted when one's right hand
Is perjured to the bosom? Proteus,
I am sorry I must never trust thee more,
But count the world a stranger for thy sake.
The private wound is deepest. O, time most   75
    accursed,
'Mongst all foes that a friend should be the worst!

78. **confounds:** i.e., confound, destroy

79. **hearty:** heartfelt, sincere

81. **tender 't:** offer it (as a **ransom** [line 80])

82. **commit:** offend

83. **paid:** satisfied (but also with the sense of accepting the offered **ransom**)

84. **receive thee honest:** i.e., accept you as honorable

86. **nor of:** neither of

88. **plain:** clear, candid, without reserve; **free:** generous

93. **wag:** fellow, boy; **how now:** an interjection meaning "how is it now?"

100. **How:** an interjection meaning "what"

102. **cry you mercy:** a phrase of apology

104. **this ring:** i.e., **the ring I gave to Julia** (line 101); **depart:** departure

PROTEUS   My shame and guilt confounds me.
　Forgive me, Valentine. If hearty sorrow
　Be a sufficient ransom for offense,   80
　I tender 't here. I do as truly suffer
　As e'er I did commit.
VALENTINE   Then I am paid,
　And once again I do receive thee honest.
　Who by repentance is not satisfied   85
　Is nor of heaven nor earth, for these are pleased;
　By penitence th' Eternal's wrath's appeased.
　And that my love may appear plain and free,
　All that was mine in Sylvia I give thee.
JULIA, ⌐aside⌐
　O me unhappy!   ⌐*She swoons.*⌐   90
PROTEUS   Look to the boy.
VALENTINE   Why, boy!
　Why, wag, how now? What's the matter? Look up.
　Speak.
JULIA, ⌐*as Sebastian*⌐   O, good sir, my master charged   95
　me to deliver a ring to Madam Sylvia, which out of
　my neglect was never done.
PROTEUS   Where is that ring, boy?
JULIA, ⌐*as Sebastian*⌐   Here 'tis; this is it.
                          ⌐*She rises, and hands him a ring.*⌐
PROTEUS   How, let me see.   100
　Why, this is the ring I gave to Julia.
JULIA, ⌐*as Sebastian*⌐
　O, cry you mercy, sir, I have mistook.
　This is the ring you sent to Sylvia.
                          ⌐*She offers another ring.*⌐
PROTEUS
　But how cam'st thou by this ring? At my depart
　I gave this unto Julia.   105
JULIA
　And Julia herself did give it me,
　And Julia herself hath brought it hither.
                          ⌐*She reveals herself.*⌐

109. **gave aim to:** i.e., was the target of (The archery metaphor underlies lines 109–11. See below.)

110. **entertained:** cherished

111. **cleft the root:** pierced the bottom of my heart (with a sense also of "cleaving the pin" [hitting the bull's-eye] in archery)   **root:** heart-root

112. **habit:** apparel, costume

114. **immodest raiment:** A woman's legs would ordinarily be covered by her long skirt, rather than being exposed as in a page's tights.

115. **of love:** i.e., put on for love's sake

117. **shapes:** appearances

123. **falls off:** i.e., revolts, withdraws its allegiance

125. **with a constant eye:** i.e., if I am constant

128. **close:** union

Aiming for the bull's-eye. (5.4.109–11)
From Gilles Corrozet, *Hecatongraphie* . . . (1543).

PROTEUS   How? Julia!

JULIA

Behold her that gave aim to all thy oaths
And entertained 'em deeply in her heart.   110
How oft hast thou with perjury cleft the root!
O, Proteus, let this habit make thee blush.
Be thou ashamed that I have took upon me
Such an immodest raiment, if shame live
In a disguise of love.   115
It is the lesser blot, modesty finds,
Women to change their shapes than men their minds.

PROTEUS

"Than men their minds"? 'Tis true. O heaven, were
    man
But constant, he were perfect; that one error   120
Fills him with faults, makes him run through all th'
    sins;
Inconstancy falls off ere it begins.
What is in Sylvia's face but I may spy
More fresh in Julia's, with a constant eye?   125

VALENTINE, ⌜*to Julia and Proteus*⌝   Come, come, a
    hand from either.
Let me be blest to make this happy close.
'Twere pity two such friends should be long foes.
    ⌜*Valentine joins the hands of Julia and Proteus.*⌝

PROTEUS

Bear witness, heaven, I have my wish forever.   130

JULIA

And I mine.

        ⌜*Enter*⌝ *Thurio, Duke,* ⌜*and*⌝ *Outlaws.*

OUTLAWS   A prize, a prize, a prize!

VALENTINE

Forbear, forbear, I say. It is my lord the Duke.
        ⌜*The Outlaws release the Duke and Thurio.*⌝
Your Grace is welcome to a man disgraced,
Banished Valentine.   135

138. **give back:** retreat, stand back

139. **measure:** reach (a fencing term)

149. **make such means:** take such measures, make such an effort

150. **conditions:** provisions, stipulations (i.e., that he must **endanger his body** by fighting for her)

154. **griefs:** grievances

155. **repeal thee home:** i.e., call you home

156. **Plead . . . merit:** perhaps, argue that the **unrivaled merit** you have shown here has created **a new** situation

157. **To which . . . subscribe:** i.e., the force and validity of which I thus acknowledge

163. **thine own:** i.e., your own **sake**

164. **kept withal:** i.e., lived with, associated with

DUKE
Sir Valentine?
THURIO   Yonder is Sylvia, and Sylvia's mine.
VALENTINE
Thurio, give back, or else embrace thy death;
Come not within the measure of my wrath.
Do not name Sylvia thine; if once again,   140
Verona shall not hold thee. Here she stands;
Take but possession of her with a touch—
I dare thee but to breathe upon my love!
THURIO
Sir Valentine, I care not for her, I.
I hold him but a fool that will endanger   145
His body for a girl that loves him not.
I claim her not, and therefore she is thine.
DUKE
The more degenerate and base art thou
To make such means for her as thou hast done,
And leave her on such slight conditions.—   150
Now, by the honor of my ancestry,
I do applaud thy spirit, Valentine,
And think thee worthy of an empress' love.
Know, then, I here forget all former griefs,
Cancel all grudge, repeal thee home again,   155
Plead a new state in thy unrivaled merit,
To which I thus subscribe: Sir Valentine,
Thou art a gentleman, and well derived;
Take thou thy Sylvia, for thou hast deserved her.
VALENTINE
I thank your Grace, the gift hath made me happy.   160
I now beseech you, for your daughter's sake,
To grant one boon that I shall ask of you.
DUKE
I grant it for thine own, whate'er it be.
VALENTINE
These banished men, that I have kept withal,

165. **endued with:** possessed of
171. **Dispose of:** i.e., make arrangements for
172. **include all jars:** bring to a close all discord
173. **triumphs:** pageants; **solemnity:** festivities
182. **That:** so that; **fortunèd:** happened
184. **discoverèd:** disclosed
186. **house:** household

A marriage feast. (5.4.185–86)
From Theodor Graminaeus, *Beschreibung derer
fürstlicher güligscher . . .* (1587).

Are men endued with worthy qualities. 165
Forgive them what they have committed here,
And let them be recalled from their exile;
They are reformèd, civil, full of good,
And fit for great employment, worthy lord.

DUKE
Thou hast prevailed; I pardon them and thee. 170
Dispose of them as thou know'st their deserts.
Come, let us go; we will include all jars
With triumphs, mirth, and rare solemnity.

VALENTINE
And as we walk along, I dare be bold
With our discourse to make your Grace to smile. 175
⌈*Pointing to Julia.*⌉ What think you of this page, my
    lord?

DUKE
I think the boy hath grace in him; he blushes.

VALENTINE
I warrant you, my lord, more grace than boy.

DUKE   What mean you by that saying? 180

VALENTINE
Please you, I'll tell you as we pass along,
That you will wonder what hath fortunèd.—
Come, Proteus, 'tis your penance but to hear
The story of your loves discoverèd.
That done, our day of marriage shall be yours, 185
One feast, one house, one mutual happiness.

They exit.

Longer Notes

1.1.81–82. **my horns are his horns, whether I wake or sleep:** Many editors think that this line is, in effect, a joke about the cuckold's **horns**—i.e., the **horns** that supposedly grow on the forehead of a husband whose wife is unfaithful. Since neither Proteus nor Speed is married, it is hard to see the point of such a joke. It seems to us more likely that in the context of dialogue about sheep and lost shepherds ("Indeed a sheep doth very often stray, / An if the shepherd be awhile away," lines 76–77), the link Speed makes between **horns** and **sleep** points more immediately to the nursery rhyme "Little Boy Blue," to which Shakespeare would later allude in *King Lear*. "Little Boy Blue" reads as follows:

Little Boy Blue, come blow your **horn.**
The sheep's in the meadow, the cow's in the corn.
But where is the boy who looks after the **sheep?**
He's under the haycock, fast **asleep.**

In *King Lear* 3.6, Shakespeare has Edgar, as Poor Tom, sing:

Sleepest or wakest, thou jolly shepherd?
Thy sheep be in the corn.
And for one blast of thy minikin mouth,
Thy sheep shall take no harm.

The *Oxford Dictionary of Nursery Rhymes* (1951) points out the *King Lear* allusion (though not the less obvious one in *Two Gentlemen of Verona*)

189

1.1.99. **laced mutton:** Some editors note that in the next scene the text describes Julia's maid as having received the letter, and argue that the "laced mutton" reference therefore describes Lucetta. However, the dialogue in the present scene makes clear that Speed is describing a meeting with Julia. See especially lines 138–43. In this early play, such discrepancies are not unusual.

1.2.98. **sharp:** Some editors believe that Lucetta puns on this musical term to refer to some harsh action of Julia's. They suggest, for example, that at line 94 Lucetta may refuse to let Julia have the paper, and that Julia hits or pinches her at line 96. If this is correct, line 100, "now you are too flat," would indicate yet another harsh action.

1.3.28. **Emperor:** The ruler that Shakespeare presents as residing at the **court** in Milan is sometimes referred to in the play as an **emperor** and sometimes as a **duke.** Editors have noted that at one time Charles V, emperor of the Holy Roman Empire, also ruled the duchy of Milan. This fact may be pertinent, or the confusion may be simply another of the inconsistencies in this early play.

2.3.29. **wold:** Our grounds for printing this emendation are detailed in Paul Werstine's review of Stanley Wells' *Re-editing Shakespeare for the Modern Reader* in *Shakespeare Studies* 19 (1987): 329–32.

2.4.20. **doublet:** The interchange in these lines about Thurio's **jerkin** being in fact a **doublet** can be interpreted in at least two ways. Janet Arnold, an expert in the clothing of the Elizabethan period, sees it as evidence that the two kinds of coats were sometimes almost indistinguishable. Writing about paintings that show "jerkins, sleeveless and worn over the doublet for extra warmth," she notes that "it is often difficult to detect the jerkin worn over a matching doublet when all the buttons are fastened." She then turns to this play: "Even their wearers in the sixteenth century found difficulty in distinguishing the two garments. Valentine mistakes Thurio's **jerkin** for a **doublet** in *The Two Gentlemen of Verona* and turns his error into a punning joke" *(Patterns of Fashion: The Cut and Construction of Clothes for Men and Women, c. 1560–1620* [New York: Drama Book, 1991], p. 70).

The other interpretation involves the possibility that Valentine deliberately calls the **doublet** a **jerkin.** Janet Winter and Carolyn Savoy point out that "The **jerkin** can be a shapeless vest worn by a peasant or a form-fitting heavily bejeweled garment, differing from a **doublet** only in its lack of sleeves" *(Elizabethan Costuming for the Years 1550–1580,* 2nd ed. [Oakland, Calif.: Other Times Publications, 1987], p. 43). Because Shakespeare so often associates the jerkin with the lower classes, Valentine's calling Thurio's coat a jerkin may be, in fact, an insult to which Thurio responds indignantly.

3.2.79. **leviathans:** Even though biblical scholars today note that the references to the leviathan in the Book of Job and in Psalms describe a variety of real or imagined creatures, including the crocodile, the marginal comments in the Geneva Bible (London, 1560) make it clear that in the sixteenth century the leviathan was equated with the whale.

Job 40.20, for example, reads "Canst thou draw out Leviathan [margin: "meaning, the whale"] with an hook . . . ?"

Job 41.1 reads "By the greatness of this monster Leviathan God showeth his greatness, and his power, which nothing can resist. None is so fierce that dare stir him up. Who is he then that can stand before me?" [margin: "If none dare stand against a whale, which is but a creature, who is able to compare with God the Creator?"]

Psalm 104.25–26 reads "So is this sea great and wide: for therein are things creeping innumerable, both small beasts and great. There go the ships, yea, that Leviathan [margin: "or, whale"] whom thou hast made to play therein."

Textual Notes

The reading of the present text appears to the left of the square bracket. Unless otherwise noted, the reading to the left of the bracket is from **F**, the First Folio text (upon which this edition is based). The earliest sources of readings not in F are indicated as follows: **F2** is the Second Folio of 1632; **F3** is the Third Folio of 1663–64; **F4** is the Fourth Folio of 1685; **Ed.** is an earlier editor of Shakespeare, beginning with Rowe in 1709. No sources are given for emendations of punctuation or for corrections of obvious typographical errors, like turned letters that produce no known word. **SD** means stage direction; **SP** means speech heading; *uncorr.* means the first or uncorrected state of the First Folio; *corr.* means the second or corrected state of the First Folio; ~ stands in place of a word already quoted before the square bracket; ∧ indicates the omission of a punctuation mark.

1.1　　　　 0. SD *Enter . . . Proteus.*] Ed.; *Valentine: Protheus,* and *Speed.* F
　　　　　 2. wits.] ~, F
　　　　　 13. travel] F (trauaile)
　　　　　 49. love ∧] Loue; F *uncorr.*; ~, F *corr.*
　　　　　 59. *and hereafter.* Milan] F (*Millaine*)
　　　　　 66. more;] F *corr.*; ~: F *uncorr.*
　　　　　 67. leave] Ed.; loue F
　　　　　 67. all,] all∧ F
　　　　　 68. metamorphosed] F (metamorphis'd)
　　　　　 70. nought] F *corr.*; naught F *uncorr.*
　　　　　 79. a] F2; *omit* F

	147.	testerned] F2; cestern'd F
1.2	5.	parle] F (par'le)
	10.	knight∧] ~, F
	56.	fool] F ('foole)
	85–86.	tune, . . . note.] ~: . . . ~, F
	88.	o'] *O*, F
	103.	your] F2; you F
	146.	will 't] F (wilt)
1.3	0.	SD *Enter Antonio and Pantino.*] *Enter Antonio and Panthino. Protheus.* F
	17.	travel] F (trauaile)
	51.	O] F2; *Pro.* Oh F
	77.	Pantino] *Panthmo* F
	89.	father] F2; Fathers F
	92.	SD *They exit.*] *Exeunt. Finis.* F
2.1	0.	SD *Enter . . . glove.*] *Enter Valentine, Speed, Siluia.* F
	20.	malcontent] F (Male-content)
	30–31.	metamorphosed] F (Metamor-phis'd)
	53.	fair∧ as, of you,] ~, ~ (~ ~) F
	81.	bed.] ~, F
	113.	stead] F (steed)
	135.	SD *Sylvia*] F (*Sil.*)
	145.	What,] ~ ∧ F
2.2	0.	SD *Enter Proteus and Julia.*] *Enter Protheus, Julia, Panthion* F
2.3	0.	SD *Enter Lance, . . . Crab.*] *Enter Launce, Panthion.* F
	29.	wold] Ed.; would F
39, 40, 42, 54.	tied] F (tide)
2.4	0.	SD *Enter . . . Speed.*] *Enter Valentine, Siluia, Thurio, Speed, Duke, Protheus.* F
	11.	Haply] F (Hap'ly)
	63.	conversed] F (conuerst)

108. mistress] F2; a Mistresse F
117. SP SERVANT] Ed.; *Thur.* F
164. too] F (to)
173. makes] F2; make F
186. ∧thou . . . jealousy.∧] (~ . . . ~.) F
201. SD *Valentine and Speed exit.*] Ed.;
     Exit. F, *1 line earlier*
203. another,] ~. F
206. Is it mine eye] Ed.; It is mine F
224. SD *He exits.*] F2; *Exeunt.* F

2.5 39. that] F2; that that F
3.1   0. SD *Enter Duke, Thurio, and Proteus.*]
          Enter Duke, Thurio, Protheus, Val-
          entine, Launce, Speed. F
          6. your] yonr F
         42. presently,] ~. F
         56. tenor] F (tenure)
         83. nought] F (naught)
        196. 'tis] t'is F
        207. you—] ~. F
   222, 226. banishèd] banish'd F
        231. them,] ~∧ F
     298–99. grandmother] F *corr.* (Grand-
             mother); Grand-mother F *uncorr.*
        300. Try] F *corr.* (try); thy F *uncorr.*
        301. Saint] F (S.)
        308. *sew*] Ed.; sowe F
        309. so?] F *corr.* (so?); so. F *uncorr.*
        319. *nameless*] F *corr.*; name lesse F
             uncorr.
        323. follow] F *corr.*; *followes* F *uncorr.*
        325. *kissed*] Ed.; *omit* F
        326. *breath*] F *corr.*; breth F *uncorr.*
        333. talk] F *corr.* (talke); take F *uncorr.*
        335. villain] F *corr.* (villaine); villanie F
             uncorr.

340. ta'en] t'ane F
342. love] F *corr.* (loue); lone F *uncorr.*
353. *hair*] F *corr.* (haire); haires F *uncorr.*
356. mine∧ twice∧] ~, ~∧ F *corr.*; ~∧~, F
    uncorr.
356. last] F *corr.*; *omit* F *uncorr.*
359. be;] ~∧ F
360. therefore] F *corr.*; Iherefore F *uncorr.*
369. impossible—] ~. F
378. long∧] F *uncorr.*; ~, F *corr.*
378. going∧] F *corr.*; ~, F *uncorr.*
380. Pox] F ('pox)
383. SD *He exits.*] Ed.; *Exeunt.* F

3.2
 1. you ∧] F *corr.*; ~, F *uncorr.*
12. gone?] F *corr.* (gon?); gon. F *uncorr.*
13. SP PROTEUS] F *corr.* (Pro.); *omit* F
    uncorr.
14. grievously] F *corr.*; heauily F *uncorr.*
47. aught] F (ought)

4.1
 0. SD *Enter certain Outlaws.*] *Enter Val-*
    entine, Speed, and certaine Out-
    lawes. F
 7. friends—] ~. F
34. travel] F (trauaile)
35. miserable] F2; often miserable F
49. An heir and near∧] Ed.; And heire
    and Neece, F
58. want—] ~. F

4.2
 0. SD *Enter Proteus.*] *Enter Protheus,*
    Thurio, Iulia, Host, Musitian,
    Siluia. F
 2. Thurio.] ~, F
28. you're] F (your')
40. hear 'em] F (heare'm)
41. SP PROTEUS] Ed.; *no SP* F
90. even] F (eu'n)

120. his] F2; her F
4.3   0. SD *Enter Eglamour.*] *Enter Eglamore, Siluia.* F
42. Recking] Ed.; Wreaking F
4.4   0. SD *Enter . . . Crab.*] *Enter Launce, Protheus, Iulia, Siluia.* F
72. thou] F2; thee F
76. to] F2; not F
158–59. is; . . . well,] ~, . . . ~; F
177. Theseus'] F (*Thesus*)
205–6. myself∧ . . . god?] ~? . . . ~. F
216. SD *She exits.*] F2; *Exeunt.* F
5.1   0. SD *Enter Eglamour.*] *Enter Eglamoure, Siluia.* F
5.2   0. SD *Enter . . . Sebastian.*] *Enter Thurio, Protheus, Iulia, Duke.* F
7. SP JULIA] Ed.; *Pro.* F
13. SP JULIA] Ed.; *Thu.* F
18. your] F4; you F
46. stand∧] ~, F
55. Sylvia's] *Siluas* F
58. *She exits.*] Ed.; *Exeunt.* F
5.4   0. SD *Enter Valentine.*] *Enter Valentine, Protheus, Siluia, Iulia, Duke, Thurio, Out-lawes.* F
5. nightingale's] F (Nightingales)
6. distresses] distrestes F
26. this∧] ~? F
59. arms'] F (armes)
115. love.] ~? F
132. SP OUTLAWS] F (*Out-l.*)

The Two Gentlemen of Verona:
A Modern Perspective

Jeffrey Masten

> . . . they used not only one board, but one bed,
> one book (if so be it they thought not one too
> many). . . . [A]ll things went in common between
> them, which all men accounted commendable.
>
> —John Lyly, *Euphues* (1579)

Within the space of about thirty lines, the final scene of
The Two Gentlemen of Verona includes the attempted
rape of one of its heroines, her rescue by her male lover,
and his forgiveness of the rapist, who also happens to be
his best friend. In love with Valentine's beloved Sylvia,
Proteus attempts to rape her; Valentine intervenes and
vows never again to trust him. But Proteus begs forgiveness:

> My shame and guilt confounds me.
> Forgive me, Valentine. If hearty sorrow
> Be a sufficient ransom for offense,
> I tender 't here. I do as truly suffer
> As e'er I did commit.
>
> (5.4.78–82)

And Valentine relents, pronounces himself "satisfied"
with Proteus' "repentance," and—shockingly, at least
to modern eyes—goes on to give the beloved Sylvia *back*
to the repentant rapist from whom he has just saved her:
"that my love may appear plain and free, / All that was
mine in Sylvia I give thee" (88–89).

This highly charged moment is perhaps the hardest to assimilate or understand from a modern perspective; indeed, it has been a locus of discontent for many of the play's twentieth-century critics and may be a reason for the play's apparent unpopularity. Writing early in the twentieth century, Arthur Quiller-Couch famously remarked that "there are, by this time, *no* gentlemen in Verona."[1] Quiller-Couch's notion of gentlemanliness is no doubt more Edwardian than Elizabethan, but he nevertheless unwittingly points to at least one of the difficulties facing twentieth-century readers and audiences when he notes that the play is part of a convention "of refining, idealising, exalting [friendship] out of all proportion, *or at any rate above the proportion it bears, in our modern minds*, either to love between man and woman or to parental love" (p. xv, my emphasis). The resulting scene in the play, he argues, represents "a flaw too unnatural to be charged upon Shakespeare" (p. vii). Quiller-Couch's terms can both give us insight into what is at stake in this scene and this play for a modern audience and suggest how to read it more clearly from the perspective of the culture within which Shakespeare lived, read, and wrote. For what may seem "unnatural" or "flaw[ed]" from a certain modern perspective is the way the play's conclusion seems to elevate its central same-sex relationship over male-female marriage. The problem is compounded by the play's use of the same rhetoric, the same terminology, for same-sex "friendship" and cross-sex "love"; characters of both sexes are interchangeably "friends" and "lovers."[2]

Until recently, for many critics the idea that Shakespeare might have written scenes that speak homoeroticism, or might have valued same-sex relations, has seemed incomprehensible; in the case of *Two Gentlemen of Verona*, a number of solutions have been proposed to absolve him of responsibility in this regard.

The play is said to demonstrate that it falls very early in Shakespeare's writing career (in this view, Shakespeare becomes a well-meaning but clumsy apprentice). Or the play is Shakespeare's parody of literature in which friendship is portrayed as greater than love (in this view, Shakespeare is intentionally clumsy).[3] Or the play's final scene, "so destructive of the relationships of the characters as they have been developed," is said to be a part of the Folio text's "maze of contradictions and inconsistencies" (here, the text is clumsy).[4] Quiller-Couch himself argues that Shakespeare originally wrote a "theatrically ineffective" scene that was revised out of the play by an unknown collaborator, who pasted in the scene we now have; nevertheless, Quiller-Couch thinks that the hypothetical scene he imagines Shakespeare first to have penned was "better, because more natural, than the text allows us to know" (p. xix). Others, likewise bothered by the apparent values of the final scene, have also proposed that the text is a collaboration.[5]

But "naturalness," to take up Quiller-Couch's terms again, may well lie in the eye and the century of the beholder; what might seem unnatural or flawed, from a standpoint that assumes the naturalness of heterosexuality as realized in a modern model of companionate marriage, may have been the *natural* structures of an earlier time and culture.

Historians of sexuality in sixteenth- and seventeenth-century England indeed have begun to show that homoerotically charged male bonds were a central aspect of this culture. While pointing out that this was a world that did not seem to divide itself along the either/or model of modern homo/heterosexuality (as an essential identity that one has and is), they have also argued, following the influential thesis of the French philosopher and historian Michel Foucault, for the existence of a set of homoerotic "practices" (along with languages that described and continued to circulate them) in early-modern England. Some of these practices were clearly condemned, including the crime of "sodomy": the term could apply to virtually any form of nonmarital, nonreproductive sexual relations, was usually associated with blasphemy or relations that crossed lines of social class, and was punishable by death. Other homoerotic practices, like male-male friendship, were condoned, celebrated, and encouraged.[6]

Male friendship was the subject of countless essays, pictorial representations, conduct books, plays, and prose fictions (like John Lyly's description of male friendship in the influential *Euphues*, quoted in the epigraph above). The language of male friendship, theorized and circulated in these texts, pervaded Shakespeare's culture in a way that may now be difficult for us to grasp—perhaps in part because the misleadingly familiar word "friend" has lost some of the intensity it had for Shakespeare and his contemporaries. Richard Brathwait, the author of the seventeenth-century conduct book *The English Gentleman*, describes friendship as a state "where two hearts are so individually united, as neither from other can well be severed";[7] in the most famous Renaissance essay on the subject (first translated into English in 1603 and republished and cited frequently), Michel de Montaigne writes that friendship

is I wot [= know] not what kind of quintessence of all this commixture [= mingling], which having seized all my will, induced the same to plunge and lose itself in his, which likewise having seized all his will, brought it to lose and plunge itself in mine, with a mutual greediness, and with a semblable concurrence [= an altogether similar running together].[8]

The closeness, intensity, and devotion of male friendship, for Montaigne as for its other Renaissance theo-
rists, is predicated on absolute identicality: friends are
"one soul in two bodies, according to the fit definition of
Aristotle" (p. 94). Again, in the words of the conduct
book, a friend is "nothing else than a *second self*, and
therefore as individuate [= indivisible] as man from
himself" (Brathwait, p. 293). Because friendship is
defined as a relationship of men equal in age, social
class, and all other attributes—a relationship that does
not allow for "difference" and "disparity" (Montaigne,
p. 92)—Montaigne explicitly excludes the possibility of
friendship with women (as well as the ancient Greek
model of same-sex pederasty, which assumed a difference of age). Because Montaigne assumes that women
are inferior to men, he views male-female friendship as
virtually unthinkable and certainly without precedent.
Moreover, he implicitly situates friendship in an upper-
class, gentlemanly world—as does Brathwait in *The
English Gentleman* (which says as much in its classmarked title). So too Edmund Spenser's *The Faerie
Queene*, which devotes one of its books to male friendship, seeks through its allegorical verse "to fashion a
gentleman or noble person in virtuous and gentle
discipline."[9] Friendship is thus relentlessly "homosocial"[10]— a relationship structured by sameness (Greek
homo-), based in the identicalness of its participants
along lines of gender and social class, and predicated on
the reproducibility of that homogeneity through imitation and emulation.

As its title emphatically suggests, *The Two Gentlemen
of Verona* stages male friendship within this decidedly
class-inflected context. Valentine and Proteus, its title(d)
protagonists, begin the play as what we might call
gentlemen-under-construction; by play's end, they have
been established as gentlemen (in a way to which we

will return). Pantino, the servant of Proteus' father
Antonio, suggests some of the possibilities for the training of young gentlemen, in language that resonates with
the gentlemanly conduct books of the period. Some
gentlemen, says Pantino,

> Put forth their sons to seek preferment out:
> Some to the wars to try their fortune there,
> Some to discover islands far away,
> Some to the studious universities.
>
> (1.3.8–11)

Repeating here the advice of yet another gentleman,
Antonio's brother, Pantino advocates travel for Proteus,
noting that it "would be great impeachment to his age /
In having known no travel in his youth" (16–17). Ac-
knowledging that his son "cannot be a perfect man, /
Not being tried and tutored in the world" (21–22),
Antonio rejects the possibility of training his son in
these exclusively male preserves, but settles on Proteus'
participation in the equally homosocial world of the
court:

> There shall he practice tilts and tournaments,
> Hear sweet discourse, converse with noblemen,
> And be in eye of every exercise
> Worthy his youth and nobleness of birth.
>
> (31–34)

The imitation and emulation that construct the
gentleman—father, uncle, and servant all agree that
Proteus must be like the sons of other men and "in eye
of every exercise"—recapitulate the identicality that
Montaigne's essay casts as a hallmark of gentlemen's
friendship. Valentine's speeches recommending Proteus to the Duke at court again make this sameness clear:

I knew him as myself, for from our infancy
We have conversed and spent our hours together[.]
. . . .
He is complete in feature and in mind,
With all good grace to grace a gentleman.

                    (2.4.62–63, 73–74)

And yet, although the play emphasizes these all-male networks and the identicalness of male friends that seems to accompany them (Valentine announces Proteus as his "second self" here), *Two Gentlemen of Verona*, as we have already seen, constantly appears to place same-sex and cross-sex relationships in direct competition.[11] As the play begins, in the middle of just such a conversation, Valentine is about to depart for the imperial court—leaving his friend, who stays behind for love of Julia. "Cease to persuade, my loving Proteus," Valentine says,

> Home-keeping youth have ever homely wits.
> Were 't not affection chains thy tender days
> To the sweet glances of thy honored love,
> I rather would entreat thy company
> To see the wonders of the world abroad. . . .
>
>   (1.1.1–6)

But though the play consistently sets male friendship and male-female love at odds (and this speech only hints at the larger disruptions in the play that culminate in the rape scene), the scene, I would argue, cannot simply be understood as a contest between platonic and erotically charged relationships, for same-sex and cross-sex relations in this play speak a remarkably similar language. Valentine's phrase "my loving Proteus," for example, gestures in both directions (Valentine loves Proteus; Proteus loves Julia). And

Proteus is "chained" by affection for Julia but equally bound to his male friend, to whom he speaks in similarly affectionate language:

Wilt thou be gone? Sweet Valentine, adieu.
Think on thy Proteus when thou haply seest
Some rare noteworthy object in thy travel.
Wish me partaker in thy happiness
When thou dost meet good hap; and in thy danger,
If ever danger do environ thee,
Commend thy grievance to my holy prayers,
For I will be thy beadsman, Valentine.

(11–18)

From its opening conversation, then, the play speaks in the intense, devotional language of male friendship. "Sweet" is used as a term of affection between the friends not only in this speech but also at 2.4.161, and is echoed in the conversation of the male lovers Patroclus and Achilles in Shakespeare's *Troilus and Cressida* (3.3.222). "Sweet Valentine" suggests the resonant historical meaning of that name, "a sweetheart, lover, or special friend" chosen on St. Valentine's Day (*Oxford English Dictionary*), and Proteus no sooner speaks than he gives himself ("*thy* Proteus") to Valentine. Likewise, Proteus and Valentine's devotion is associated in the opening lines of the play with an erotic tale of love, that between Hero and Leander. The allusion to this "love-book" works, again, in the direction of both same-sex and cross-sex affection:

VALENTINE
   And on a love-book [you will] pray for my success?
PROTEUS
   Upon some book I love I'll pray for thee.

VALENTINE
>That's on some shallow story of deep love,
>How young Leander crossed the Hellespont.

PROTEUS
>That's a deep story of a deeper love,
>For he was more than over shoes in love.

>(19–24)

Christopher Marlowe's erotic narrative *Hero and Leander*, a poem that Shakespeare seems to have read in manuscript, features both the relationship of its title (Leander attempts the prodigious feat of swimming the Hellespont to be with his beloved Hero) *and* a significant homoerotic component (the sea-god Neptune attempts to seduce Leander during his journey). Once *Hero and Leander* was published in 1598, playgoers could hear the two friends, with their playful punning on "deep," citing this heteroerotic poem at arguably its most homoerotic moment: Leander's underwater encounter with Neptune and the seductions of the god's "deep persuading oratory."[12]

If the opening scene of the play thus both gestures toward the importance of two kinds of love and puts them in competition, that competition is only heightened by the play's staging of the friends' identicalness when Proteus falls for Valentine's beloved Sylvia. Yet Proteus, in the first of two important speeches attempting to negotiate the competing demands of friendship and love, demonstrates the extent to which again the two speak in identical terms:

>Is it mine eye, or Valentine's praise,
>Her true perfection, or my false transgression,
>That makes me reasonless to reason thus?

. . . .

> Methinks my zeal to Valentine is cold,
> And that I love him not as I was wont.
> O, but I love his lady too too much,
> And that's the reason I love him so little.
>
> (2.4.206–16)

Even as Proteus has difficulty distinguishing his own feelings from Valentine's (and thus presents his similarity to Valentine yet again), the speech plays out the contention of two "loves" and turns on the currency of that word in both relationships.

Proteus' next solo speech (separated from the first by a short comic scene) again compares his loves—"To leave my Julia, shall I be forsworn. / To love fair Sylvia, shall I be forsworn. / To wrong my friend, I shall be much forsworn" (2.6.1–3)—and in its inversion of syntax (shall I/I shall) seems to privilege the demands of friendship. (The point is even stronger in the Folio text of the play, which places question marks after each of the first two lines.) The speech continues to demonstrate the intersecting languages of love and friendship, but it also plays with and puts pressure on the theory of friendship we have seen outlined in Montaigne:

> I cannot leave to love, and yet I do.
> But there I leave to love where I should love.
> Julia I lose, and Valentine I lose;
> If I keep them, I needs must lose myself;
> If I lose them, thus find I by their loss:
> For Valentine, myself; for Julia, Sylvia.
> I to myself am dearer than a friend.
>
> (17–23)

Montaigne writes of his friend, "If a man urge me to tell wherefore I loved him, I feel it cannot be expressed but by answering; Because it was he, because it was my self"

(p. 92); this formulation demonstrates succinctly how Proteus' speech uses but inverts the principles of Renaissance friendship. In deciding "I to myself am dearer than a friend," Proteus double crosses the friend who is supposed to be "as individuate as man from himself." Losing that friend, he ostensibly finds himself: "I cannot now prove constant to myself / Without some treachery used to Valentine" (2.6.31–32). But despite all his revisions, Proteus grounds his betrayal of his friend in the language of friendship. Like the previous speech, this one turns on the use of a single word in the languages of both kinds of love: "Valentine I'll hold an enemy, / Aiming at Sylvia as a sweeter *friend*" (29–30, my emphasis). This line demonstrates the extent to which love and friendship in *Two Gentlemen of Verona* are constantly collapsing into and substituting for one another; though they would seem to be most at odds in Proteus' betrayal of Valentine for Sylvia, even here they cannot be entirely differentiated. Abandoning Valentine ("Sweet Valentine, adieu"), Proteus, in his duplicity, chooses Sylvia as a "sweeter friend"—*and thus becomes more like Valentine*. And when Valentine is later banished from court, Proteus assures him that he can address his letters to Sylvia to/through him.

The circulation of letters in this play (like the circulation of rings) is complex and significant,[13] and contributes to themes we have been examining. We can notice, for example, that several of the letters, though "about" male-female love, trace in their movements the outline of male relations. Early in the play, Julia writes a letter to Proteus, who, interrupted in its reading by his father, says:

> 'tis a word or two
> Of commendations sent from Valentine,

> Delivered by a friend that came from him.
> . . . .
> There is no news, my lord, but that he writes
> How happily he lives, how well beloved
> And daily gracèd by the Emperor,
> Wishing me with him, partner of his fortune.
> (1.3.53–60)

The letter from the lover becomes a letter from the loving friend. Delivered by yet another friend, said to be about friendship, and narrated to his father, it leads to Proteus' following the course of his friend Valentine to court.

The doubling of Valentine at the court is accomplished by letter even before Proteus leaves Verona. In the very next scene, Sylvia causes Valentine to write a letter for her to a "secret, nameless friend of [hers]" (2.1.105), who is Valentine himself. His servant Speed explains, in a speech that culminates in elaborately doubling rhetoric: *"Herself* hath taught *her love himself* to write unto *her lover"* (2.1.172–73, my emphasis). As Jonathan Goldberg observes, Sylvia "can only speak to her lover if he speaks for her" (p. 72), and we thus see how the structures of letter writing in the play both trace a circuit of relations between men (Valentine writes to himself) and often preclude the speaking/writing of women (in a way that is only too legible in the rape scene). Valentine becomes (to use Speed's terms) both Sylvia's "pupil" and her "tutor"; a "spokesman" to and for himself, he is both "scribe" and recipient of a desire that he writes himself—a desire therefore difficult to see as fully "Sylvia's" (2.1.141, 143, 150). A friend is a second self, and this letter then may be the play's most witty figuration of the letter as a fundamentally homosocial text: a letter between *man.*

Thus the larger problem of *Two Gentlemen of Verona* is its placing of male friendship and male-female love in competition, all the while reluctant either to differentiate or to hierarchize them. (They speak an overlapping language; they can apparently be substituted for and translated into one another; the culture values both.) Its final scene, with which we began, seeks to resolve this dilemma. The crux of Valentine's speech forgiving Proteus for the attempted rape of Sylvia brings together again the rhetorics of love and friendship:

> I am paid,
> And once again I do receive thee honest.
> . . . .
> And that my love may appear plain and free,
> All that was mine in Sylvia I give thee.
> (5.4.83–89)

Valentine's statement—so extraordinary to modern eyes—demonstrates at this climactic moment the inclusion of cross-sex love within the bonds of male friendship. In this transaction, in exchange for Proteus' "ransom" of "hearty sorrow" for his transgression, Valentine receives Proteus back as "honest" (meaning "trustworthy," but also "chaste"). And, in the ambidextrous syntax of the speech's concluding couplet, he both gives Proteus all that he owns in Sylvia (i.e., he gives Sylvia to Proteus) *and* transfers all his love in Sylvia to Proteus.

It is significant that Proteus' "Forgive me, Valentine" and Valentine's "I am paid" combine to figure the rape as a transgression against Valentine, not Sylvia. Indeed, this scene of rape, apology, and forgiveness is central to the play's ongoing project, the construction of Valentine and Proteus as gentlemen. Valentine had earlier been banished from the court by Sylvia's father for a transgression of the gentlemanly code that is not unlike Proteus'. Valentine's literally upwardly mobile plot to climb a ladder in order to steal away an upper-class woman against her father's wishes (even if not against her will) had led to his being labeled, in heavily classmarked rhetoric, a *"base* intruder, overweening *slave"* (3.1.161, my emphasis)—no *gentle*man of Verona. But Valentine's magnanimity in this final scene makes possible his reinstatement as a gentleman, soon after he has successfully interrupted Proteus' similar transgression of the gentlemanly code. The Duke announces:

> Know, then, I here forget all former griefs,
> Cancel all grudge, repeal thee home again,
> Plead a new state in thy unrivaled merit,
> To which I thus subscribe: Sir Valentine,
> Thou art a gentleman, and well derived;
> Take thou thy Sylvia, for thou hast deserved her.
>
> (5.4.154–59)

By literally granting Valentine a new (e)state—the status of gentleman, a position in the state of gentlemen the Duke rules, and the inheritance of that estate/state through Sylvia—the Duke's "subscribing" literally writes Valentine back into the male world of the court, restoring him from outlaw status. In an act of naming similar to that performed by the title of the play itself, the Duke here makes Valentine a gentleman, (re)names him "Sir Valentine."

That Valentine can be decreed "well derived" and declared a gentleman at the end of the play (after he had apparently been one all along, according to the play's title and text) may suggest the way in which *Two Gentlemen of Verona* mystifies or sidesteps the increasing tensions in sixteenth- and seventeenth-century England over social mobility—over whether gentlemen were *born* (ancestrally derived) or *made*. Like the gentlemen's conduct books, this play was first written, acted, and published during a period of remarkable social mobility, a time when the boundary between gentlemen and common men was increasingly fluid and contested.[14] Furthermore, conduct books both describe gentility and enable its replication and proliferation, often among the very members of society from whom the books' writers sought to distinguish themselves.[15] (From the perspective of twentieth-century American culture, which—in theory, at least—subscribes to the idea that merit is based not on birth but on achievement through education and work, this may not seem a controversial idea; for Elizabethans, it was.) Far from shoring up, protecting, and prescribing the behavior of proper gentlemen, conduct books might well produce more of them, or more who aspired to this status. Indeed, Shakespeare himself was probably a beneficiary of this kind of upward mobility: in 1596, possibly with the help of his increasingly prosperous playwright-actor son, Shakespeare's father acquired a coat of arms that signaled his entrance into the gentry. A number of seventeenth-century title pages list William Shakespeare as a "Gent."

Seeing the play as a kind of staged conduct book (illustrating the do's and don'ts of proper gentlemanly behavior) may make sense of an odd moment in 4.1 when Valentine is apprehended by "certain Outlaws" in the forest. "Have you the tongues?" they ask him, eager to know of his ability with languages, and he replies, "My youthful travel therein made me happy." This convinces the outlaws that "[t]his fellow were a king for our wild faction"; even outlaws in this universe apparently value the humanistic learning of a gentleman (33–37). In the final scene, Valentine's retraining as a

gentleman—presumably demonstrated to the audience's satisfaction by his having rescued Sylvia and
stood up to the coward Thurio—enables him to plead
successfully that these men (some of whom turn out to
have been gentlemen with transgressions remarkably
similar to Valentine's own) be welcomed back into civil
society. They too are "endued with worthy qualities . . .
reformèd, civil, full of good, / And fit for great employment" (5.4.165–69). Insofar as the play stages the
(re)education, the (re)training of gentlemen and their
establishment in positions of power and prestige, we
would not want to underestimate the power of this
performance itself as a "conduct book" for the six-
teenth- and seventeenth-century audiences who wit-
nessed it on stage and page.

The reintegration of the outlaws is part of the sustained restoration of the play's homosocial power structure, a system no longer seen to be in competition with
cross-sex love and marriage but indeed surrounding and
underwriting it. Earlier in the scene, following Proteus'
self-recognizing confession of "inconstancy," Valentine
had brought Julia and Proteus back together in a gesture
that (through the multiple referents of the word
"friend") had also simultaneously reconstructed the
two men's friendship:

> Come, come, a hand from either.
> Let me be blest to make this happy close.
> 'Twere pity two such friends should be long foes.
>   (5.4.126–29)

The play concludes in a similar fashion, placing cross-
sex joining in the context of same-sex reunion. Though
the play's standard comic ending gestures toward a
double marriage, the pairing of male-female couples

receives relatively little emphasis. Just as the play had begun with friendly conversation between men, it concludes with an all-male exchange among the Duke, Valentine, and Proteus; by the last lines of *Two Gentlemen of Verona*, the women in question have virtually disappeared from view. Though Sylvia is not herself violated like Philomela, the mythological victim from Ovid's *Metamorphoses* invoked in the figure of the nightingale at the beginning of the scene (5.4.5), her silence nevertheless mirrors Philomela's literal loss of tongue: Sylvia speaks no lines after the attempted rape. Julia is (silently) present in boy's clothing.[16] Indeed, as if to register the picture of a relentlessly male world all the more completely, Valentine offers up the still-disguised Julia to the unknowing Duke as an object of male-male admiration: "What think you of this page, my lord?"

DUKE
   I think the boy hath grace in him; he blushes.
VALENTINE
   I warrant you, my lord, more grace than boy.
DUKE   What mean you by that saying?
                                          (5.4.176–80)

With Valentine promising the Duke an offstage answer to his dangling question (if not a boy, is the page a man? a woman?), the play ends with Valentine and Proteus conversing about their marriage(s) in lines that only make more ambiguous the question of what or who are being joined in the play's concluding couplings: "our day of marriage," Valentine says to his friend, "shall be yours, / One feast, one house, one mutual happiness" (5.4.185–86). Though the play had insistently staged friendship and cross-sex love as mutually exclusive alternatives, friendship between men is restored *through* (not at the cost of) marriage to women. And, in the persistent unification and mutuality of the play's final line (recalling *Euphues'* "one board, . . . one bed, one book"), the two gentlemen are once again, to quote the gentlemanly conduct book, "no less selfly than sociably united" (Brathwait, frontispiece).

To be sure, the play does stage some resistance to this apparently monolithic conclusion. Proteus' fluctuations in love and friendship are ridiculed even in his name, for example. There are as well the significant figures of Lance and Speed, the gentlemen's servants. Speed, arguably the wittiest and shrewdest character in the play, takes a jaundiced view of both male friendship and male-female love. He sees the letters that crisscross the plot of the play not as bearers of crucial emotional information or persuasion but as commodities within a service economy: "Sir, I could perceive nothing at all from her, no, not so much as a ducat for delivering your letter" (1.1.138–39). Lance's monologues with (to?) his dog Crab likewise refigure and parody both the male-female relations in the play (in a scene of leave-taking, the dog "sheds not a tear nor speaks a word" [2.3.33], just as Julia had taken her leave "without a word" in the previous scene [2.2.17]) and possibly the male friend as second self ("I am the dog. No, the dog is himself, and I am the dog. O, the dog is me, and I am myself. Ay, so, so" [2.3.22–24]). Moreover, the play includes Julia, apparently the first cross-dressing, male-initiative-seizing heroine of Shakespeare's writing career.[17] And, in the lyrics of the striking song sung to Sylvia in 4.2, we may even hear a suggestion that she (as enigma and as otherworldly beauty) is not only the object but also the *source* of the identical desires of the male friends and courtiers: "Who is Sylvia? What is she, / That *all* our swains commend her?" (4.2.41–42, my emphasis). Still, we should note that the song in context is a complicated homosocial performance (Proteus substitutes for Valentine, while singing for Thurio), to be settled only in the renegotiation of friendship among swains in the final scene.

From a certain modern perspective, then, the ending of the play may not make sense, for we are in the modern scheme generally used to thinking of heterosexuality and homosexuality as mutually exclusive, with each of these terms designating something fundamental about an individual's identity. But if we assume instead a social system in which marriage (a version of marriage that often subordinates and silences women) and the homoeroticism of male friendship coexist, we can begin to understand what transpires in *Two Gentlemen of Verona*. Yet to see the possibility of this kind of homoeroticism in the play, to cut it loose from the modern sense of "homosexuality" (and of "heterosexuality" as well), is not necessarily to read a play in which male-male relations have a radical or disruptive edge (as perhaps in Christopher Marlowe's roughly contemporaneous depiction of intense male friendship in *Edward II*). As I hope I have made clear, this analysis of friendship seems to provide very little liberatory potential for women in particular (we might want to compare Portia's position in *The Merchant of Venice*—another play that puts in tension male friendship and male-female love, worked out in part through a more active ring-bearing, cross-dressed female heroine). The disruption may, nevertheless, come in the critical act of *reading* from a revised modern perspective—in the act of reading or watching the play at some remove from its characters and the world they enact. The play doesn't necessarily give us (where "us" includes modern read ers who are female and male, straight and gay, and middle-, lower-, and upper-class) a fully recognizable place to identify ourselves. But thinking about its decidedly different configuration of sexual and social relationships—a world in which same-sex and cross-sex relations coexist, a world in which marriage is not the only culturally sanctioned value—may allow us a space for reimagining, through one representation of Shakespeare's world, our own.

———————

1. Arthur Quiller-Couch, introduction to *The Two Gentlemen of Verona*, ed. Quiller-Couch and John Dover Wilson, New Shakespeare (Cambridge: Cambridge University Press; New York: Macmillan, 1921), p. xiv. Subsequent citations will be parenthetical.

2. An extended version of the argument in this essay appears in chapter 2 of my *Textual Intercourse: Collaboration, Authorship, and Sexualities in Renaissance Drama* (Cambridge: Cambridge University Press, 1997).

3. See Hereward T. Price, "Shakespeare as Critic," *Philological Quarterly* 20 (1941): 390–99. Clifford Leech's introduction to the Arden edition of the play (London: Methuen, 1969) largely concurs with this view (p. lxxiv).

4. Anne Barton, introduction to *The Two Gentlemen of Verona*, in *The Riverside Shakespeare*, ed. G. Blakemore Evans et al. (New York: Houghton Mifflin, 1974), p. 143.

5. Recently critics and scholars have been much more willing to see Shakespeare working within the predominantly collaborative context of the Renaissance theater; indeed, his other "two gentlemen" play, *The Two Noble Kinsmen* (1613)—a play that may be the other bookend to his career and is remarkably similar in

its themes—was certainly written with a collaborator, John Fletcher. But collaboration, a common practice in Shakespeare's theater, need not be seen as inevitably producing flawed plays; see Gerald Eades Bentley, *The Profession of Dramatist in Shakespeare's Time, 1590–1642* (Princeton: Princeton University Press, 1971); Stephen Orgel, "What Is a Text?" in *Staging the Renaissance: Reinterpretations of Elizabethan and Jacobean Drama,* ed. David Scott Kastan and Peter Stallybrass (New York: Routledge, 1991), pp. 83–87; Jeffrey A. Masten, "Beaumont and/or Fletcher: Collaboration and the Interpretation of Renaissance Drama," *ELH* 59 (1992): 337–56.

6. See Michel Foucault, *The History of Sexuality,* vol. 1, *An Introduction,* trans. Robert Hurley (New York: Vintage, 1980). The best essay on sodomy and friendship in this period is historian Alan Bray's "Homosexuality and the Signs of Male Friendship in Elizabethan England," in *Queering the Renaissance,* ed. Jonathan Goldberg (Durham: Duke University Press, 1993), pp. 40–61. See also Bray's *Homosexuality in Renaissance England* (London: Gay Men's Press, 1982).

7. Richard Brathwait, *The English Gentleman* (London: by John Haviland [for] Robert Bostock, 1630), p. 243. Subsequent citations will be parenthetical. The spelling of all early-modern works quoted in this essay has been modernized.

8. Michel de Montaigne, *The Essayes Or Morall, Politike and Millitairie Discourses of Lo: Michaell de Montaigne ... now done into English,* trans. John Florio (London: by Val. Sims for Edward Blount, 1603), p. 93. Subsequent citations to this edition will be parenthetical. For a modern reprint of Florio's translation, which Shakespeare read, see *The Essays of Montaigne,* with an introduction by George Saintsbury, 3 vols. (London: David Nutt, 1892; reprint. New York: AMS, 1967).

9. Edmund Spenser, "A Letter of the Authors Expounding his Whole Intention . . . ," in *The Faerie Queene*, ed. Thomas P. Roche, Jr. (New Haven: Yale University Press, 1981), p. 15. See Ruth Kelso's extensive bibliography of conduct books, *The Doctrine of the English Gentleman in the Sixteenth Century* (Gloucester, Mass.: Peter Smith, 1964). Lauren J. Mills, *One Soule in Bodies Twain: Friendship in Tudor Literature and Stuart Drama* (Bloomington, Ind.: Principia, 1937), surveys the wide expanse of Renaissance friendship literature and its classical precedents.

10. This influential term was coined by queer theorist Eve Kosofsky Sedgwick; see *Between Men: English Literature and Male Homosocial Desire* (New York: Columbia University Press, 1985).

11. I avoid the terms *heterosexual* and *homosexual* throughout this essay, for, as David Halperin demonstrates, both terms have only a very recent history and fit poorly with earlier conceptions of sexuality and identity. See Halperin, *One Hundred Years of Homosexuality and Other Essays on Greek Love* (New York: Routledge, 1990), pp. 17–18.

12. Christopher Marlowe, *Hero and Leander*, in *The Complete Works of Christopher Marlowe*, ed. Fredson Bowers, vol. 2 (Cambridge: Cambridge University Press, 1973), 2.226.

13. On letters and their significance for determining identity in the play, see Jonathan Goldberg, "Shakespearian Characters: The Generation of Silvia," in *Voice Terminal Echo: Postmodernism and English Renaissance Texts* (New York: Methuen, 1986), pp. 68–100. Subsequent citations will be parenthetical.

14. See, for example, Lawrence Stone, "Social Mobility in England, 1500–1700," *Past and Present* 33 (1966): 16–55.

15. This point is made in Frank Whigham's important

book on conduct literature; see especially chapter 1, "Courtesy Literature and Social Change," in *Ambition and Privilege: The Social Tropes of Elizabethan Courtesy Theory* (Berkeley: University of California Press, 1984), pp. 1–31.

16. This moment, like Julia's speech on "play[ing] the woman's part" at 4.4.169–81, gestures toward the actual performance practice in Shakespeare's theater, where boys played the parts of women. On this, see Phyllis Rackin, "Androgyny, Mimesis, and the Marriage of the Boy Heroine on the English Renaissance Stage," *PMLA* 102 (1987): 29–41. See also Jonathan Goldberg, "The Transvestite Stage," chapter 4 of *Sodometries: Renaissance Texts, Modern Sexualities* (Stanford: Stanford University Press, 1992), pp. 105–43; and Stephen Orgel, *Impersonations: The Performance of Gender in Shakespeare's England* (Cambridge: Cambridge University Press, 1996).

17. It may be significant that Julia's name "Sebastian" (4.4.41)—like Rosalind's chosen male name "Ganymede" in *As You Like It*—carries with it a homoerotic allusion here to St. Sebastian. On this, see Mario DiGangi, *The Homoerotics of Early Modern Drama* (Cambridge: Cambridge University Press, 1997), pp. 20, 167.

Further Reading

The Two Gentlemen of Verona

Abbreviations: *TGV=The Two Gentlemen of Verona;
MV=The Merchant of Venice; AYL=As You Like It;
TN=Twelfth Night; Cym.=Cymbeline*

Beadle, Richard. "Crab's Pedigree." In *English Comedy*,
ed. Michael Cordner, Peter Holland, and John Kerrigan,
pp. 12–35. Cambridge: Cambridge University Press,
1994.

Beadle traces the history of the "clown-with-dog" act
that Shakespeare uses in his pairing of Lance and Crab
back to its roots in classical and medieval comedy, while
also noting the more immediate influence of sub-
literary popular entertainments available to Elizabethans. The author specifically links Crab to Labes
(Grabber), the dog arraigned for stealing a cheese in
Aristophanes' *The Wasps*, and to the solo mime's performing dog best known from the erotic farce "The
Weeping Bitch," a tale of illicit sex widely disseminated
from the twelfth century on (the ironic twist in the case
of Crab is that he does not weep). Crab's pedigree
suggests that he is heir to "an ancient line in sexual
conquest through farcical deception, the excremental
emblem of lust and defilement."

Beckerman, Bernard. "Shakespeare's Dramaturgy and
Binary Form." *Theatre Journal* 33.1 (1981): 5–17.

Using *TGV* as his test case, Beckerman argues that the
binary form of the duet constitutes Shakespeare's fa-
vored dramaturgical unit of scene construction. While
46 percent of the text explicitly calls for two players,

Beckerman finds evidence of the binary form in scenes with several characters onstage, thus bringing the total number of duologues to 71 percent of the text. Such disguised duets include trios in which a third figure either remains mute (Pantino in 1.3.46–78) or serves as the audience's surrogate through choric asides that comment on the actual duet figures (Speed in 2.1.94–144). Even the quintet scene in which three outlaws encounter Valentine and Speed (4.1) is a duet in its presentational structure since the multiple outlaws are virtually interchangeable or "redundant" in their interrogation of Valentine. The binary form also provides a dramaturgical explanation for Sylvia's silence in the controversial final scene. By keeping Sylvia and Julia mute through the duet between Valentine and Proteus (5.4.63–89) and Sylvia silent through the duet between Proteus and Julia (90–125), Shakespeare "assure[s] concentration of effect" and "maintains presentational focus and the vigor that goes with it."

Bradbrook, Muriel C. "The Fashioning of a Courtier." In *Shakespeare and Elizabethan Poetry: A Study of His Earlier Work in Relation to the Poetry of the Time*, pp. 141–61, esp. 147–54. London: Chatto and Windus, 1951.

Bradbrook's examination of *TGV* in the context of the courtly love tradition and the education of a courtier as found in Castiglione's *Book of the Courtier* leads her to conclude that the play "is a study of manners rather than of sentiments, of behaviour rather than emotion." Friendship, the dominant theme, emerges as the more "personal" relationship; love remains the "courtly," artificial one. The "germ" of the play is found in the exchange (5.4.63–89) between Valentine and Proteus in which Proteus asks for forgiveness and Valentine re-

sponds, "Then I am paid." By releasing Sylvia to Proteus, Valentine demonstrates "in transcendent form"
what was for Castiglione "the first and greatest virtue of
a gentleman": namely, the courtly virtue of magnanimity. Sylvia's silence necessarily follows, for she is simply
"the prize." Recognition of the priority of the friendship
code and the fashioning of the perfect gentleman over
the tenets of Petrarchan wooing prevents a misunder-
standing of the play's conclusion.

Brooks, Harold F. "Two Clowns in a Comedy (to say
nothing of the Dog): Speed, Launce (and Crab) in *The
Two Gentlemen of Verona*." *Essays and Studies*, n.s. 16
(1963): 91–100.
  In an essay that is widely regarded as a classic in *TGV*
scholarship, Brooks demonstrates that the low comic
characters—Speed, Lance, and Crab—while not essential to the cause-effect needs of plot, contribute to the
play's thematic unity by providing a network of comic
parallels that parody the main themes of friendship and
love. Speed in his "cut and thrust" with Valentine in 2.1
wittily exposes the "love is blind" theme, while Lance in
his self-sacrifice and love for Crab burlesques Valentine's friendship with Proteus and Julia's love for him.
In a comment that anticipates the full-length argument
of Beadle (see above), Brooks finds a parodic link
between Proteus as lover and Crab as gift: neither is
worthy of Sylvia.

Bullough, Geoffrey, ed. *"The Two Gentlemen of Verona."*
In *Narrative and Dramatic Sources of Shakespeare*, vol. 1,
pp. 203–68. 1957. Reprint, London: Routledge and
Kegan Paul; New York: Columbia University Press,
1975.
  Bullough reprints excerpts from an English transla-

tion of Jorge de Montemayor's 1542 *Diana Enamorada* (the primary source), Boccaccio's tale of Titus and Gisippus as found in Sir Thomas Elyot's *The Governour* (a possible source), and several analogues (Sir Philip Sidney's *Arcadia*, John Lyly's *Euphues*, the *Tragaedia von Julio und Hyppolita* [trans. Georgina Archer], and F. Scala's *Flavio Tradito*). The Boccaccio tale provided both the triangular relationship of two male friends in love with the same woman and the generous act of one man resigning his bride to his friend (the Valentine, Proteus, and Sylvia plot line). The *Diana*, which afforded Shakespeare the Julia plot in its detailed story of treachery to a former mistress who disguises herself as a male in pursuit of her lost lover, became Shakespeare's "text-book of amorous entanglements and sentiment." Shakespeare shows an enormous debt to themes (the conflict between love and friendship), techniques (symmetrical balancing of character), and character types (the waggish servant) made popular by Lyly in his courtly plays. Lance, who shows the influence of the rustic clown type, appears to be Shakespeare's original invention.

Castiglione, Baldesar. *The Book of the Courtier* (1528). Trans. George Bull. 1967. Reprint, Harmondsworth: Penguin Books, 1983. [An abridged translation by Friench Simpson is available through the Milestones of Thought series (1959; reprint, New York: Frederick Ungar, 1980).]

The most famous of Renaissance courtesy books, Castiglione's *The Courtier* (arranged as a series of conversations spread out over four nights in 1507 at the ducal court of Urbino) is a handbook for the fashioning of the ideal gentleman who would perfectly combine the intellectual, martial, and diplomatic skills of the consummate scholar, soldier, and statesman in worthy service to his lord. The program of education advocated the cultivation of good manners and civil discourse in pursuit of both individual excellence and social harmony. A key doctrine is *sprezzatura*—the art that (by virtue of its gracefully natural manner) conceals its artifice— often glossed as unself-conscious ease or nonchalance. In *TGV*, Pantino's proposal for Proteus' journey to the court of Milan to learn how to become the "perfect" gentleman (1.3.31–34) articulates the tenets of the courtesy book tradition as exemplified in Castiglione. (See the picture on page 32.)

Ewbank, Inga Stina. " 'Were Man But Constant, He Were Perfect': Constancy and Consistency in *The Two Gentlemen of Verona*." In *Shakespearian Comedy*, ed. Malcolm Bradbury and David Palmer, pp. 31 57. Stratford upon Avon Studies 14. London: Edward Arnold; New York: Crane, Russak, 1972.

Ewbank discusses *TGV*'s inconsistencies of plot, character, and language and concludes that both the play's problems and its "sense of life" inhere in an essential contradiction of language, a medium used to describe genuine feelings and real experiences but one that can also "falsify" what it supposedly describes. A vivid sense of "experience . . . outrun[ning] language" is particularly noticeable in the middle of the play. Relating *TGV* to Sonnet 40 ("Take All My Love"), Ewbank suggests that the sonnet does a better job of conveying something of how love "really feels" because it "work[s] through and around convention" to capture the human dimension. This dimension is notably absent from the final scene of *TGV*, whose "real inconsistency . . . is that Shakespeare is trying to use as his raw material what characters say (attitudes) rather than what they are (people)."

Friedman, Michael D. " 'To be slow in words is a woman's only virtue': Silence and Satire in *The Two Gentlemen of Verona*." *Shakespeare and Renaissance Association of West Virginia: Selected Papers* 17 (1994): 1–9.

Friedman focuses on Sylvia's plight in 5.4 in an attempt to construct a feminist performance criticism that allows for a critique of the patriarchal silencing of the comic heroine without sacrificing the comic tone associated with the endings of Shakespeare's comedies. A sampling of productions reveals a variety of staging possibilities. Instead of either cutting the potentially offensive passages or emphasizing them to expose sexist values, Friedman advocates the use of satirical laughter against the patriarchal attitudes that a feminist production of *TGV* would criticize. By choosing a gagged but vigorously struggling Sylvia, one of the productions examined serves as a model in exploiting the ending's potential for satire. The strong visual image of a woman whose silence was involuntary encouraged the audience to laugh at the "ridiculous chauvinism of the men"; the result was a theatrical reconciling of a feminist perspective with the traditional comic closure of marriage.

Girard, René. "Love Delights in Praises: Valentine and Proteus in *The Two Gentlemen of Verona*." In *A Theater of Envy*, pp. 8–20. New York: Oxford University Press, 1991. (The chapter is a revised version of an essay that first appeared in *Philosophy and Literature* 13 (1989): 231–47 under the title "Love Delights in Praises: A Reading of *The Two Gentlemen of Verona*.")

The author examines *TGV* in accordance with his theory of "mimetic" or "mediated" desire, a concept that explains the concord and discord that occur when friends inclined to imitate each other become rivals by desiring a common object that cannot be shared. In

TGV, Proteus desires Sylvia solely because "he is predisposed in favor of whatever Valentine desires," the key speech being Proteus' soliloquy at 2.4.202–24. Shakespeare is fascinated by the ambivalence of imitation: "Valentine and Proteus can be friends only by desiring alike and, if they do, they are enemies. Neither one can sacrifice friendship to love or love to friendship without sacrificing what he wants to retain and retaining what he wants to sacrifice." The offer to relinquish Sylvia to Proteus is Valentine's attempt to escape from "the mimetic double bind," but the "search for a compromise" contaminates things that should remain separate: "friendship and Eros, possessiveness and generosity, . . . love and hatred." The act of renunciation thus "becomes a parody of itself, tinged with the slipperiness of sexual perversion." Girard posits that mimetic rivalry, which gives *TGV* its plot, is "the staple" of plays and novels.

Goldberg, Jonathan. "Shakespearian Characters: The Generation of Silvia." In *Voice Terminal Echo: Postmodernism and English Renaissance Texts*, pp. 68–100, esp. 68–81. New York: Methuen, 1986.
Applying a postmodern "voice as text" theory to a play "spawn[ed]" by Ovidian metamorphoses, Goldberg analyzes the characters in *TGV* as literal figures "who voice the letters" in which their names are written. Constituted as "surfaces to be read and reread," the characters find "themselves by citing old saws [and find] each other by exchanging letters, registering loss by tearing words, deforming them as they speak, wooing by [rhetorical] figures." Since the characters are rooted in literal devices, they are "little more than marks on a page assuming their life." Sylvia (whose name comes from the Latin *silva*, or "woods") is "what her name betokens," that name being both her destiny (tho woods

she finally arrives in) and her destination ("both in *TGV* and the texts it generates"). The passage at 2.1.152–54 holds the key to her generation: "the letter—literally and figuratively." Likewise, her puzzling silence at the end has already been written in Ovid's story of Philomela, who, in moving from a father's court to a threatening forest, became a victim of male desire and lost her human voice. Valentine's destiny also lies in his name— a valentine is both a lover and a love letter—and it is no accident that Sylvia and Valentine's first scene together is played around a letter. Responding to the criticism of the characters in *TGV* as "wooden," Goldberg counters that their " 'woodenness' (literally) is the most transparent indication of the genealogy of the Shakespearian character," which in this play is inscribed in "the troping of the *silva* tradition of pastoral" and in the many allusions to Ovid.

Lindenbaum, Peter. "Education in *The Two Gentlemen of Verona.*" *Studies in English Literature 1500–1900* 15 (1975): 229–44.

According to Lindenbaum, the central theme of *TGV* is not the conflict between love and friendship but a moral education that subsumes and ultimately transcends the courtly and social kind usually emphasized by critics. Lindenbaum charts the moral development of both Valentine and Proteus by noting how the iterative word "perfect" and the thematic ideal of "the perfect gentleman" undergo a radical change in the course of the play. From being simply a matter of social grace and courtly manners (1.3.20–34), perfection comes to be understood as a moral state of religious grace and spiritual virtues (5.4.118–23). Integral to this redefinition is the spatial dynamic that shifts from Verona to Milan to the uncivilized wood. While Valentine displays minor failings in Milan, it is Proteus who becomes

"Italianate" in the worst Elizabethan sense. The journey from the court to the wood exposes both "gentlemen" as "unaccommodated men" and forces them to recognize their status as representatives of flawed humanity. In keeping with the Christian doctrine of human fallibility, the characters learn that true perfection must be "in harmony with and modeled after divine precept." For Lindenbaum, both Valentine's generous offer and Sylvia's silence in the final scene are necessary for Proteus' moral redemption. "Silvia is silent . . . because she fully understands what [Valentine] is doing."

Masten, Jeffrey. "Between Gentlemen: Homoeroticism, Collaboration, and the Discourse of Friendship." In *Textual Intercourse: Collaboration, Authorship, and Sexualities in Renaissance Drama*, pp. 28–62, csp. 37–48. Cambridge: Cambridge University Press, 1997.

Masten's discussion of *TGV* derives from his thesis that Shakespeare, like other Renaissance dramatists, "wrote within a paradigm that insistently figured writing as mutual imitation, collaboration, and homoerotic exchange." In *TGV*'s emphasis on "the homosocial networks of gentlemanly education through emulation," Masten observes an interdependence rather than an opposition between male friendship and Petrarchan love, both of which in this play "speak a remarkably similar language." Noting that Petrarchan sonnets, "though often written *to* and *about* women, . . . circulat[ed] between men . . . registering . . . courtiership as courtship," the author examines the play's negotiation of the competing demands of friendship and Petrarchan love to illuminate "the collaborative male inscription of a social order; within the play's collaborative practice, texts and women circulate among gentlemen." The final scene, in which Valentine stops Proteus' attempted rape of Sylvia and then surrenders her to Proteus, is both the "most extreme instance of contending Petrarchan love and male friendship *and* the succinct inscription of their ultimate relation." In *TGV* as in the gentlemen's conduct books of the period, "homoeroticism functions as part of the network of power; it reconstitutes and reflects the homogeneity of the gentlemanly subject." (See the picture from Richard Brathwait's *The English Gentleman* on page 36.)

Price, Hereward T. "Shakespeare as Critic." *Philological Quarterly* 20 (1941): 390–99, esp. 396–99.

According to Price, the only way to make sense of *TGV*'s strange ending is to read the play as Shakespeare's mocking exposure of the artifice associated with Renaissance codes of courtly love and friendship. The playwright was particularly "gunning for" the literary convention that established Valentine as the ideal courtly lover and that prioritized friendship between men over the love of man for woman. Shakespeare "wring[s] the last drop of silliness" out of Valentine's conventionalized behavior in the ridiculous offer of Sylvia to Proteus, "a logical development" of *TGV*'s overall satiric design. The surrender of Sylvia is sometimes cut in modern productions because the convention Shakespeare was exposing "no longer exists and therefore we do not understand the passage."

Richman, David. *Laughter, Pain, and Wonder: Shakespeare's Comedies and the Audience in the Theater*. Newark: University of Delaware Press; London: Associated University Presses, 1990.

Drawing on his own experience as a director and on the productions of others, Richman explores how Shakespeare's comedies in performance evoke a complicated mixture of laughter, pain, and wonder. In the chapters on laughter and pain, he addresses the "farcical analogy" provided by Lance and Crab and Shakespeare's experimentation with a suffering heroine (Julia) and a figure who feels some internal conflict (Proteus). Richman's most sustained treatment of the play, however, appears in the chapter on wonder, where he discusses the problematic ending (pp. 150–56). Shakespeare fails to realize the "wonder of miracle" that he intended in Valentine's magnanimous gesture and Proteus' repentance because he "still lacks sufficient power" to make credible both the gesture and the remorse. The ending's difficulties "grow out of the playwright's exploration, for the first time in drama, of a problem of evil in a context of romance." The best strategy, therefore, is to play the scene as a parody of romance.

Schlueter, June, ed. *"Two Gentlemen of Verona": Critical Essays.* New York: Garland, 1996.

The first part of this anthology (following an introductory overview of the scholarship and performance history related to *TGV*) provides eighteen critical commentaries spanning the years 1765 to 1996; the second part is devoted to eleven theater reviews dealing with productions between 1821 and 1991. Besides extracts from Samuel Johnson, William Hazlitt, Algernon Swinburne, Victor Oscar Freeburg, and Bertrand Evans, Schlueter reprints several essays annotated separately in the present "Further Reading" section (Brooks, Ewbank, Friedman, Slights, and Weimann). The remaining critical essays are S. Asa Small's "The Ending of *The Two Gentlemen of Verona*," Ralph M. Sargent's "Sir Thomas Elyot and the Integrity of *The Two Gentlemen of Verona*," Thomas A. Perry's "Proteus, Wry-Transformed Traveller," Frederick Kiefer's "Love Letters in *The Two Gentlemen of Verona*," Charles A.

Hallett's "'Metamorphising' Proteus: Reversal Strategies in *The Two Gentlemen of Verona*," Kathleen Campbell's "Shakespeare's Actors as Collaborators: Will Kempe and *The Two Gentlemen of Verona*," John Timpane's "'I am But a Foole, Looke You': Launce and the Social Functions of Humor," and Patty S. Derrick's "Feminine 'Depth' on the Nineteenth-Century Stage." In addition to nineteenth-century productions by Frederick Reynolds and Augustin Daly, the theater reviews cover revivals by Granville-Barker (1904), William Poel (1910), Michael Langham (1956), Robin Phillips (1970), Robin Phillips and David Toguri (1975), Leon Rubin (1984), Charles Newell (1990), and David Thacker (1991). Two assessments, one by Harry Keyishian and the other by Patty S. Derrick, deal with the 1983 BBC TV/Time Life production directed by Don Taylor.

Shapiro, Michael. "Bringing the Page Onstage: *The Two Gentlemen of Verona*." In *Gender in Play on the Shakespearean Stage: Boy Heroines and Female Pages*, pp. 65–91. Ann Arbor: University of Michigan Press, 1994.

Shapiro analyzes the "theatrical vibrancy" that results from Shakespeare's versatile use of cross-gendered casting (boys playing girls) and cross-gendered disguise (the female character assuming a male identity) in five plays: *TGV, MV, AYL, TN,* and *Cym.* The chapter on *TGV* focuses on Julia's disguise as the "cheeky page," Shakespeare's innovative use of the precocious boy servant popular in the court comedies of John Lyly. In the interplay of male actor/female character/male disguise, Shapiro observes not a fusion "into a single androgynous entity" but a "vertically layered richness of perception" that allows the audience to experience all three aspects at given moments; see, for example, Julia's exchanges with Lucetta (2.7.40–56) and with Sylvia (4.4.157–73) in which the male performer reflexively "underscore[s]" his presence in the layered gender identities of Julia/Sebastian. When Julia gives Proteus the wrong ring, it is the character's "moment of greatest power, a moment when the presentational and mimetic facets of his/her identity, the male actor's persona and the female character, coalesce to enable the boy heroine to seize control of the play."

Slights, Camille Wells. *"The Two Gentlemen of Verona* and the Courtesy Book Tradition." *Shakespeare Studies* 16 (1983): 13–31. Revised and reprinted as "Common Courtesy in *The Two Gentlemen of Verona*." In *Shakespeare's Comic Commonwealths*, pp. 57–73. Toronto: University of Toronto Press, 1993.

Indebted to the courtesy book tradition, specifically the courtly program of education advocated by Castiglione, *TGV* is neither an unequivocal endorsement of conventional codes of friendship and love nor a parody of such conventions. An understanding of the Renaissance concern with the formation of the perfect or complete gentleman sheds light on the widely criticized last scene. As a result of the journey to the wood where they are exposed to raw nature and the violence of outlaws, Valentine and Proteus come to the shocking realization that a misguided courtly education, with its emphasis on the superficial, can degenerate into a brutality not all that different from the savagery of the wild. Valentine's controversial gesture to surrender Sylvia to her would-be rapist offers Proteus a way back to the world of civilized society "where a gentleman's word is his bond but where gentlemen characteristically communicate through indirection." Valentine assumes that Proteus will understand and accept the offer. Like Lindenbaum (see above), Slights reads Sylvia's silence as a sign of her complicity in Valentine's strategy. For Slights, however, both the gesture and the silence are

required for Proteus' *social* rather than moral reclama-
tion. *TGV*, Shakespeare's contribution to the courtesy
book tradition, "presents courtly elegance as a positive
value, [but] it also shows us how fragile and easily
corrupted this ideal is."

Weimann, Robert. "Laughing with the Audience: *The
Two Gentlemen of Verona* and the Popular Tradition of
Comedy." *Shakespeare Survey* 22 (1969): 35–42.
   Arguing that Shakespeare favors laughter "with" rather than "at" in his comedies, Weimann draws on the
social structure of the Elizabethan popular theater in
his examination of three devices that contribute to this
type of laughter in *TGV*: asides to an audience that
believes in the speaker's comic commentary; direct
address to an audience in which the speaker becomes
"the clowning object and laughing subject of his own
mirth and that of the audience"; and disguise, since the
"disguised person is usually laughed with, not at."
Speed's asides in 2.1 in which he mocks the "high-
flown" rhetoric of Sylvia and Valentine are examples of
the first, Lance's leave-taking in 2.3 illustrates the second, and Julia's disguise exemplifies the third. The
rapport or "comic concurrence" between audience and
actor-character encouraged by these techniques results
in "a wider comic vision through which the [play's]
main theme of friendship and courtly love . . . is dra-
matically controlled and comically evaluated."

Shakespeare's Language

Abbott, E. A. *A Shakespearian Grammar*. New York:
Haskell House, 1972.
   This compact reference book, first published in 1870,
helps with many difficulties in Shakespeare's language.

It systematically accounts for a host of differences between Shakespeare's usage and sentence structure and our own.

Blake, Norman. *Shakespeare's Language: An Introduction.* New York: St. Martin's Press, 1983.
This general introduction to Elizabethan English discusses various aspects of the language of Shakespeare and his contemporaries, offering possible meanings for hundreds of ambiguous constructions.

Dobson, E. J. *English Pronunciation, 1500–1700.* 2 vols. Oxford: Clarendon Press, 1968.
This long and technical work includes chapters on spelling (and its reformation), phonetics, stressed vowels, and consonants in early modern English.

Houston, John. *Shakespearean Sentences: A Study in Style and Syntax.* Baton Rouge: Louisiana State University Press, 1988.
Houston studies Shakespeare's stylistic choices, considering matters such as sentence length and the relative positions of subject, verb, and direct object. Examining plays throughout the canon in a roughly chronological, developmental order, he analyzes how sentence structure is used in setting tone, in characterization, and for other dramatic purposes.

Onions, C. T. *A Shakespeare Glossary.* Oxford: Clarendon Press, 1986.
This revised edition updates Onions' standard, selective glossary of words and phrases in Shakespeare's plays that are now obsolete, archaic, or obscure.

Robinson, Randal. *Unlocking Shakespeare's Language: Help for the Teacher and Student.* Urbana, Ill.: National

Council of Teachers of English and the ERIC Clearing-
house on Reading and Communication Skills, 1989.

Specifically designed for the high-school and under-
graduate college teacher and student, Robinson's book
addresses the problems that most often hinder present-
day readers of Shakespeare. Through work with his own
students, Robinson found that many readers today are
particularly puzzled by such stylistic devices as subject-
verb inversion, interrupted structures, and compres-
sion. He shows how our own colloquial language con-
tains comparable structures, and thus helps students
recognize such structures when they find them in
Shakespeare's plays. This book supplies worksheets—
with examples from major plays—to illuminate and
remedy such problems as unusual sequences of words
and the separation of related parts of sentences.

Williams, Gordon. *A Dictionary of Sexual Language and
Imagery in Shakespearean and Stuart Literature*. 3 vols.
London: Athlone Press, 1994.

Williams provides a comprehensive list of the words
to which Shakespeare, his contemporaries, and later
Stuart writers gave sexual meanings. He supports his
identification of these meanings by extensive quota-
tions.

Shakespeare's Life

Baldwin, T. W. *William Shakspere's Petty School*. Urbana: University of Illinois Press, 1943.

Baldwin here investigates the theory and practice of
the petty school, the first level of education in Elizabethan England. He focuses on that educational system
primarily as it is reflected in Shakespeare's art.

Baldwin, T. W. *William Shakspere's Small Latine and Lesse Greeke.* 2 vols. Urbana: University of Illinois Press, 1944.

Baldwin attacks the view that Shakespeare was an uneducated genius—a view that had been dominant among Shakespeareans since the eighteenth century. Instead, Baldwin shows, the educational system of Shakespeare's time would have given the playwright a strong background in the classics, and there is much in the plays that shows how Shakespeare benefited from such an education.

Beier, A. L., and Roger Finlay, eds. *London 1500–1700: The Making of the Metropolis.* New York: Longman, 1986.

Focusing on the economic and social history of early modern London, these collected essays probe aspects of metropolitan life, including "Population and Disease," "Commerce and Manufacture," and "Society and Change."

Bentley, G. E. *Shakespeare's Life: A Biographical Handbook.* New Haven. Yale University Press, 1961.

This "just-the-facts" account presents the surviving documents of Shakespeare's life against an Elizabethan background.

Chambers, E. K. *William Shakespeare: A Study of Facts and Problems.* 2 vols. Oxford: Clarendon Press, 1930.

Analyzing in great detail the scant historical data, Chambers' complex, scholarly study considers the nature of the texts in which Shakespeare's work is preserved.

Cressy, David. *Education in Tudor and Stuart England.* London: Edward Arnold, 1975.

This volume collects sixteenth-, seventeenth-, and early-eighteenth-century documents detailing aspects of formal education in England, such as the curriculum, the control and organization of education, and the education of women.

De Grazia, Margreta. *Shakespeare Verbatim: The Reproduction of Authenticity and the 1790 Apparatus.* Oxford: Clarendon Press, 1991.

De Grazia traces and discusses the development of such editorial criteria as authenticity, historical periodization, factual biography, chronological development, and close reading, locating as the point of origin Edmond Malone's 1790 edition of Shakespeare's works. There are interesting chapters on the First Folio and on the "legendary" versus the "documented" Shakespeare.

Dutton, Richard. *William Shakespeare: A Literary Life.* New York: St. Martin's Press, 1989.

Not a biography in the traditional sense, Dutton's very readable work nevertheless "follows the contours of Shakespeare's life" as he examines Shakespeare's career as playwright and poet, with consideration of his patrons, theatrical associations, and audience.

Fraser, Russell. *Young Shakespeare.* New York: Columbia University Press, 1988.

Fraser focuses on Shakespeare's first thirty years, paying attention simultaneously to his life and art.

Schoenbaum, S. *William Shakespeare: A Compact Documentary Life.* New York: Oxford University Press, 1977.

This standard biography economically presents the essential documents from Shakespeare's time in an accessible narrative account of the playwright's life.

Shakespeare's Theater

Bentley, G. E. *The Profession of Player in Shakespeare's Time, 1590–1642*. Princeton: Princeton University Press, 1984.

Bentley readably sets forth a wealth of evidence about performance in Shakespeare's time, with special attention to the relations between player and company, and the business of casting, managing, and touring.

Berry, Herbert. *Shakespeare's Playhouses*. New York: AMS Press, 1987.

Berry's six essays collected here discuss (with illustrations) varying aspects of the four playhouses in which Shakespeare had a financial stake: the Theatre in Shoreditch, the Blackfriars, and the first and second Globe.

Cook, Ann Jennalie. *The Privileged Playgoers of Shakespeare's London*. Princeton: Princeton University Press, 1981.

Cook's work argues, on the basis of sociological, economic, and documentary evidence, that Shakespeare's audience—and the audience for English Renaissance drama generally—consisted mainly of the "privileged."

Greg, W. W. *Dramatic Documents from the Elizabethan Playhouses*. 2 vols. Oxford: Clarendon Press, 1931.

Greg itemizes and briefly describes many of the play manuscripts that survive from the period 1590 to around 1660, including, among other things, players' parts. His second volume offers facsimiles of selected manuscripts.

Gurr, Andrew. *Playgoing in Shakespeare's London*. Cambridge: Cambridge University Press, 1987.

Gurr charts how the theatrical enterprise developed from its modest beginnings in the late 1560s to become a thriving institution in the 1600s. He argues that there were important changes over the period 1567–1644 in the playhouses, the audience, and the plays.

Harbage, Alfred. *Shakespeare's Audience.* New York: Columbia University Press, 1941.

Harbage investigates the fragmentary surviving evidence to interpret the size, composition, and behavior of Shakespeare's audience.

Hattaway, Michael. *Elizabethan Popular Theatre: Plays in Performance.* London: Routledge & Kegan Paul, 1982.

Beginning with a study of the popular drama of the late Elizabethan age—a description of the stages, performance conditions, and acting of the period—this volume concludes with an analysis of five well-known plays of the 1590s, one of them (*Titus Andronicus*) by Shakespeare.

Shapiro, Michael. *Children of the Revels: The Boy Companies of Shakespeare's Time and Their Plays.* New York: Columbia University Press, 1977.

Shapiro chronicles the history of the amateur and quasi-professional child companies that flourished in London at the end of Elizabeth's reign and the beginning of James'.

The Publication of Shakespeare's Plays

Blayney, Peter. *The First Folio of Shakespeare.* Hanover, Md.: Folger, 1991.

Blayney's accessible account of the printing and later life of the First Folio—an amply illustrated catalog to a

1991 Folger Shakespeare Library exhibition—analyzes the mechanical production of the First Folio, describing how the Folio was made, by whom and for whom, how much it cost, and its ups and downs (or, rather, downs and ups) since its printing in 1623.

Hinman, Charlton. *The Norton Facsimile: The First Folio of Shakespeare*. 2nd ed. New York: W. W. Norton, 1996.
   This facsimile presents a photographic reproduction of an "ideal" copy of the First Folio of Shakespeare; Hinman attempts to represent each page in its most fully corrected state. The second edition includes an important new introduction by Peter Blayney.

Hinman, Charlton. *The Printing and Proof-Reading of the First Folio of Shakespeare*. 2 vols. Oxford: Clarendon Press, 1963.
   In the most arduous study of a single book ever undertaken, Hinman attempts to reconstruct how the Shakespeare First Folio of 1623 was set into type and run off the press, sheet by sheet. He also provides almost all the known variations in readings from copy to copy.

Key to
Famous Lines and Phrases

Home-keeping youth have ever homely wits.
                    [*Valentine*—1.1.2]

I have no other but a woman's reason:
I think him so because I think him so.
                    [*Lucetta*—1.2.23–24]

They do not love that do not show their love.
                    [*Julia*—1.2.31]

The uncertain glory of an April day. [*Proteus*—1.3.86]

What light is light if Sylvia be not seen?
What joy is joy if Sylvia be not by—
Unless it be to think that she is by
And feed upon the shadow of perfection?
                    [*Valentine*—3.1.178–81]

                              . . . love
Will creep in service where it cannot go.
                    [*Proteus*—4.2.20–21]

Who is Sylvia? What is she . . .   [*Song*—4.2.41–55]

How use doth breed a habit in a man!
                    [*Valentine*—5.4.1]

FOLGER SHAKESPEARE LIBRARY

The world's leading center for Shakespeare studies presents acclaimed editions of Shakespeare's plays.

Hamlet
0-7434-7712-X

A Midsummer Night's Dream
0-7434-7754-5

Julius Caesar
0-7434-8274-3

King Lear
0-7434-8276-X

Much Ado About Nothing
0-7434-8275-1

Macbeth
0-7434-7710-3

Othello
0-7434-7755-3

The Merchant of Venice
0-7434-7756-1

Romeo and Juliet
0-7434-7711-1

For a complete list of Folger Shakespeare Library Editions, visit www.simonsays.com